TACACS+: Advanced Access Management in Networks

James Relington

DEDICATION

To those who seek knowledge, inspiration, and new perspectives—
may this book be a companion on your journey, a spark for curiosity,
and a reminder that every page turned is a step toward discovery.

AKNOWLEDGEMENTS

I would like to express my deepest gratitude to everyone who contributed to the creation of this book. To my colleagues and mentors, your insights and expertise have been invaluable. A special thank you to my family and friends for their unwavering support and encouragement throughout this journey.

Introduction to TACACS+

In the world of network security and access control, few protocols have maintained their relevance and critical role like TACACS+. Terminal Access Controller Access-Control System Plus, commonly known as TACACS+, has been a cornerstone in providing secure authentication, authorization, and accounting (AAA) services within enterprise and service provider networks. As organizations have expanded their IT infrastructures and adopted more complex, multi-vendor environments, the demand for reliable and flexible access control mechanisms has surged, making TACACS+ an indispensable tool for network administrators and security professionals.

TACACS+ originated as an enhancement over its predecessors, TACACS and Extended TACACS (XTACACS), designed to address the growing need for a more robust and secure protocol. Initially developed by Cisco Systems, TACACS+ quickly gained traction for its versatility and advanced security features. Unlike its predecessors, TACACS+ leverages the Transmission Control Protocol (TCP) for transport, providing a more reliable connection-oriented approach compared to the User Datagram Protocol (UDP) used by RADIUS, its closest counterpart. This shift to TCP allows TACACS+ to offer better delivery assurance, making it particularly suitable for environments where packet loss or transmission errors could compromise security or disrupt operations.

One of the distinguishing characteristics of TACACS+ is its ability to separate the AAA components into independent processes. While RADIUS combines authentication and authorization into a single function, TACACS+ divides these elements into discrete transactions. This modular approach grants network administrators greater control and granularity when defining user access policies. By handling authentication, authorization, and accounting separately, TACACS+ allows for more precise policy enforcement and enhances flexibility when managing diverse network devices, including routers, switches, firewalls, and wireless access points.

The authentication process in TACACS+ ensures that only verified users can access network resources. When a user initiates a connection to a network device, TACACS+ validates the credentials against a centralized user database. This centralized approach simplifies user management and strengthens security by reducing the reliance on local device-based user accounts. Furthermore, TACACS+ supports multiple authentication methods, including passwords, tokens, and certificates, aligning with modern multi-factor authentication (MFA) strategies. This adaptability helps organizations meet stringent security requirements and regulatory compliance mandates.

Authorization within TACACS+ defines what actions an authenticated user is permitted to perform on network devices. This is a critical component in enforcing least privilege principles, ensuring that users only have access to the commands and resources necessary for their role. For example, a network technician may be granted read-only access to configuration files, while a senior engineer might have full administrative privileges. By specifying granular command authorizations, TACACS+ minimizes the risk of accidental misconfigurations or intentional misuse of network resources.

Accounting, the third pillar of TACACS+, records user activity and session data, providing valuable insight into network usage and security events. TACACS+ accounting logs capture details such as login times, executed commands, session durations, and logout events. This audit trail is essential for forensic investigations, compliance reporting, and overall network visibility. Security teams rely on these logs to detect anomalies, investigate incidents, and demonstrate adherence to industry standards and legal requirements.

Security is a fundamental concern in access control, and TACACS+ addresses this through its full encryption of communication between clients (network devices) and the TACACS+ server. Unlike RADIUS, which only encrypts user credentials while leaving other elements in plaintext, TACACS+ encrypts the entire payload. This added layer of security protects sensitive information such as user commands and accounting data from being intercepted or manipulated during transmission. As cyber threats grow more sophisticated, this comprehensive encryption model strengthens network defenses against common attacks like man-in-the-middle (MITM) and packet sniffing.

Another compelling advantage of TACACS+ is its vendor-neutral design. While it was initially created by Cisco, TACACS+ has become widely adopted across various network equipment manufacturers. Its interoperability enables seamless integration in heterogeneous network environments, reducing operational complexity and promoting consistency in access control across different platforms. This makes TACACS+ particularly valuable for organizations that deploy equipment from multiple vendors and need a unified solution for AAA services.

As enterprises evolve towards hybrid and cloud-native architectures, the relevance of TACACS+ continues to expand. The protocol is highly adaptable and can be integrated into both on-premises and cloud-based infrastructures. In hybrid environments where traditional data centers coexist with public and private clouds, TACACS+ ensures consistent access policies are enforced regardless of where network assets are located. Its compatibility with modern identity and access management (IAM) systems, such as LDAP and Active Directory, further enhances its utility in contemporary IT ecosystems.

Network administrators often appreciate TACACS+ for its detailed logging and debugging capabilities, which simplify troubleshooting and incident response. When configuring TACACS+ servers and clients, administrators can review extensive logs that highlight authentication errors, authorization denials, or accounting discrepancies. These logs provide actionable insights that streamline problem resolution and strengthen the overall security posture of the network.

The significance of TACACS+ extends beyond technical functionality. It embodies a proactive approach to security governance and risk management. By centralizing AAA functions, TACACS+ helps organizations establish standardized policies and procedures for controlling user access. This standardization reduces human error, supports operational efficiency, and cultivates a security-conscious culture within the IT department. Whether deployed in small businesses or global enterprises, TACACS+ serves as a vital safeguard, ensuring that access to critical network resources is tightly controlled and continuously monitored.

The protocol's enduring presence in network security is a testament to its reliability, scalability, and adaptability. As the digital landscape continues to change with the emergence of new technologies and evolving cyber threats, TACACS+ remains a trusted ally for securing network access and enforcing robust security controls. Its combination of modular AAA functions, comprehensive encryption, and wide interoperability positions TACACS+ as a crucial component in the defense-in-depth strategy of any organization.

The Evolution of Network Access Control

The history of network access control is a reflection of how technology and security have evolved hand in hand. In the early days of computing, networks were closed environments, typically isolated to a single organization or even a single building. Access control was rudimentary, often relying on simple passwords or even physical access restrictions to terminals. There was little concern about external threats because networks were not connected to larger systems. However, as networking technologies advanced and organizations began linking their systems through wide area networks and eventually the internet, the need for stronger, more sophisticated access control mechanisms became apparent.

The first significant shift occurred with the rise of mainframe and client-server architectures, where multiple users needed to access centralized resources. Passwords remained the primary method of authentication, but the introduction of centralized user databases allowed administrators to manage credentials more efficiently. Systems like UNIX began using local password files, and authentication was tightly bound to the device or operating system in use. However, this model presented serious limitations as networks expanded and the number of users and devices grew. Administrators faced challenges in managing disparate sets of credentials across multiple systems, leading to inconsistencies and vulnerabilities.

As organizations began deploying larger and more distributed networks, early forms of remote access protocols like Telnet and FTP emerged. These protocols allowed users to connect to remote systems, but they did so without encryption, transmitting credentials in plaintext across networks. This exposed sensitive information to potential interception, prompting the search for more secure solutions. The introduction of protocols such as SSH (Secure Shell) improved the confidentiality of remote access sessions by encrypting traffic, but there was still a need for a standardized approach to authentication, authorization, and accounting that could operate across diverse devices and network segments.

In response to these growing demands, early access control protocols such as TACACS (Terminal Access Controller Access-Control System) and RADIUS (Remote Authentication Dial-In User Service) were developed. TACACS, introduced by the U.S. Department of Defense, provided a method for authenticating users accessing ARPANET resources. However, its capabilities were basic, focusing primarily on authentication without robust support for authorization or accounting. RADIUS, developed later by Livingston Enterprises, introduced a more comprehensive AAA framework. It became widely adopted for managing dial-up connections and wireless networks, offering basic user authentication and centralized management of network access policies.

Despite its popularity, RADIUS had limitations, particularly in environments where more granular control over user actions was necessary. RADIUS combined authentication and authorization into a single process, limiting the flexibility administrators had in defining access permissions. Additionally, RADIUS used UDP as its transport protocol, which, while efficient, lacked the reliability and flow control mechanisms of TCP. Furthermore, RADIUS only encrypted user credentials, leaving other parts of its packets in plaintext, a concern as cyber threats became more sophisticated.

The next phase in the evolution came with the development of TACACS+ by Cisco Systems. TACACS+ addressed many of the shortcomings found in both its predecessor TACACS and in RADIUS. By adopting TCP for transport, TACACS+ improved the reliability of message delivery. Its design separated the AAA functions into independent processes, giving administrators fine-grained control over authentication, authorization, and accounting. This modularity was particularly useful in enterprise networks where different users required different levels of access, and specific actions on network devices needed to be carefully restricted.

The adoption of TACACS+ coincided with the expansion of enterprise networks into global operations. As organizations opened branch offices, adopted remote work policies, and integrated supply chains, the perimeter of networks stretched beyond traditional boundaries. This distributed environment demanded access control solutions that could scale easily and enforce uniform policies regardless of location or device type. TACACS+ became a preferred choice for many large enterprises and service providers, particularly those utilizing Cisco infrastructure, due to its detailed command-level authorization capabilities and comprehensive encryption of entire payloads.

Parallel to these developments, the rise of wireless networking and mobile devices introduced new complexities. Traditional wired networks had predictable points of entry, but Wi-Fi access points and mobile devices created a dynamic environment where users could connect from virtually anywhere. Network Access Control (NAC) solutions emerged to address this challenge, combining policy enforcement with health checks to ensure that only compliant devices could gain access to the network. These systems leveraged protocols like RADIUS in conjunction with agents and posture assessments to verify device configurations, patch levels, and security settings before granting access.

As virtualization, cloud computing, and software-defined networking (SDN) gained traction, network access control had to adapt once again. Organizations moved critical workloads to cloud platforms and hybrid environments, where traditional perimeter-based security models were no longer sufficient. The concept of Zero Trust Architecture (ZTA) emerged, advocating that no user or device, whether inside or outside the corporate network, should be automatically trusted. This paradigm shift reinforced the need for stronger identity and access management solutions, including the use of TACACS+ for securing administrative access to virtualized network infrastructure and cloud-hosted services.

Today, network access control continues to evolve in response to emerging technologies such as the Internet of Things (IoT) and edge computing. The proliferation of connected devices, many with limited or no native security features, has expanded the attack surface for organizations. Modern NAC solutions now integrate machine learning and artificial intelligence to detect anomalies, enforce adaptive policies, and provide real-time responses to threats. However, the foundational principles laid by protocols like TACACS+ remain relevant, ensuring that human and machine identities are properly authenticated and authorized before interacting with critical network components.

The journey from simple password-based access to complex, context-aware access control systems reflects the increasing sophistication of both networks and the threats they face. While the tools and protocols have changed, the underlying objective has remained consistent: to protect sensitive information and critical infrastructure by ensuring that only trusted users and devices can interact with network resources. TACACS+, as part of this broader narrative, represents a significant milestone in the continuous effort to build secure, resilient, and manageable networks in an ever-changing technological landscape.

TACACS+ vs. RADIUS: A Comparative Overview

TACACS+ and RADIUS stand as two of the most widely implemented protocols for network access control. Both play crucial roles in the authentication, authorization, and accounting processes within enterprise networks, yet they approach these tasks with differing philosophies and architectures. Understanding the differences between TACACS+ and RADIUS is essential for network engineers and security professionals tasked with designing and managing secure, scalable, and efficient network environments. While both protocols serve the same fundamental purpose of providing AAA services, their distinct characteristics make each better suited to particular scenarios.

TACACS+, developed by Cisco Systems, was designed as an enhancement to the original TACACS and XTACACS protocols. One of its most notable features is its use of the TCP transport protocol, which establishes a reliable, connection-oriented session between the client and the server. This ensures that packets are delivered in order and that errors can be retransmitted, which adds a layer of reliability in environments where packet loss is a concern. By contrast, RADIUS, developed by Livingston Enterprises, utilizes the UDP transport protocol. UDP is connectionless, which means it does not guarantee packet delivery or order. While this makes RADIUS faster and less resource-intensive in low-latency, high-speed networks, it can also result in reliability issues in networks prone to packet drops.

Another key distinction lies in how each protocol handles the separation of AAA functions. TACACS+ fully decouples authentication, authorization, and accounting into separate processes. This allows administrators to define highly granular policies, controlling not only who can access the network but also precisely what they can do once they are authenticated. For example, TACACS+ enables command-level authorization, permitting or denying specific commands on devices such as routers, switches, and firewalls. This level of detail is particularly important in environments where strict control over device configuration and management is required, such as service provider networks or high-security enterprise environments. In contrast, RADIUS combines authentication and authorization into a single process, providing less flexibility when it comes to defining and enforcing user permissions.

Encryption is another critical area where TACACS+ and RADIUS differ. TACACS+ encrypts the entire payload of its messages, including the authentication, authorization, and accounting data. This ensures that all communication between the network device and the TACACS+ server remains confidential and protected from eavesdropping or tampering. RADIUS, on the other hand, only encrypts the password in its authentication packet, leaving other fields, such as usernames, authorization information, and accounting records, in plaintext. While the limited encryption in RADIUS may suffice for some environments, it exposes metadata and session details that could be exploited by attackers if intercepted. This makes TACACS+ the preferred choice for organizations prioritizing end-to-end encryption of sensitive network transactions.

The differences between TACACS+ and RADIUS also extend to their typical use cases. RADIUS is widely adopted in scenarios where network access is granted to end-users, such as wireless networks, VPN access, and dial-up services. Its efficiency and speed make it well-suited for large-scale deployments where rapid authentication is necessary to accommodate thousands of simultaneous connections. Wireless networks, in particular, often rely on RADIUS to authenticate users through 802.1X, which is a common standard for port-based network access control. TACACS+, on the other hand, is more commonly deployed to secure administrative access to network infrastructure. It is frequently used to control access to network devices such as routers, switches, and firewalls, where detailed control over user actions is essential to prevent configuration errors and unauthorized changes.

Another important consideration is vendor support and interoperability. RADIUS, being an open standard, is supported by virtually every major networking vendor and is integrated into a wide range of products and services. Its open nature ensures that RADIUS can be used in multi-vendor environments with minimal compatibility concerns. TACACS+, while initially developed by Cisco, has also been implemented by other vendors but remains more closely associated with Cisco-centric environments. Nevertheless, many modern systems and third-party applications now provide TACACS+ support, helping bridge gaps in heterogeneous network ecosystems.

Accounting features in both protocols provide administrators with valuable data for monitoring, auditing, and troubleshooting purposes. RADIUS accounting focuses on network usage statistics such as session start and stop times, data transferred, and connection status. This makes it useful for service providers or organizations that need to track resource consumption for billing or capacity planning. TACACS+ accounting, while similar in its ability to log session activity, goes a step further by recording detailed information on the specific commands executed by users on network devices. This facilitates more comprehensive auditing and forensic analysis, allowing security teams to reconstruct user actions in the event of a security incident or policy violation.

The choice between TACACS+ and RADIUS is often influenced by the operational priorities and specific security requirements of an organization. Enterprises that prioritize granular access control and comprehensive session encryption may favor TACACS+ to safeguard their critical network infrastructure. Organizations focused on efficiently managing large volumes of user authentications, such as those providing wireless or remote access, may lean towards RADIUS due to its speed, lightweight nature, and broad support for end-user devices and authentication mechanisms.

It is also worth noting that the two protocols can and often do coexist within the same organization. For instance, RADIUS might be employed for authenticating employees accessing Wi-Fi networks or VPN services, while TACACS+ is reserved for securing access to the organization's core network devices and infrastructure. By using both protocols in tandem, organizations can leverage the strengths of each to build a robust and layered access control framework.

As network environments continue to evolve with the rise of cloud services, remote workforces, and IoT devices, the debate between TACACS+ and RADIUS remains relevant. Security professionals must carefully assess their organizational needs, regulatory requirements, and infrastructure characteristics when deciding which protocol to implement. Both TACACS+ and RADIUS have proven to be resilient, adaptable, and essential components in the defense against unauthorized access and data breaches, each contributing uniquely to the complex landscape of modern network security.

TACACS+ Protocol Architecture

The architecture of the TACACS+ protocol is built on a foundation designed to provide reliability, flexibility, and security in managing network access. At its core, TACACS+ operates as a client-server protocol, where network devices such as routers, switches, firewalls, and wireless controllers act as clients that communicate with a centralized TACACS+ server. This server is responsible for handling all AAA functions: authentication, authorization, and accounting. The distributed nature of the architecture allows network administrators to manage access policies from a central point, eliminating the inefficiencies and security risks associated with maintaining local credentials on every device.

TACACS+ leverages the Transmission Control Protocol, or TCP, as its transport layer. This decision is significant because TCP is a connection-oriented protocol that guarantees the reliable delivery of packets. The use of TCP ensures that TACACS+ messages are transmitted in sequence and without loss, providing a dependable method of communication between clients and servers even in less-than-ideal network conditions. This reliability is critical in enterprise environments where administrative actions on network devices must be securely and consistently transmitted to prevent configuration errors or service disruptions. The protocol typically operates over TCP port 49, which is reserved exclusively for TACACS+ communication, simplifying firewall and security policy configurations.

The modular structure of TACACS+ distinguishes it from other AAA protocols by separating the three core functions into discrete processes. When a network device initiates a TACACS+ session, it does not bundle authentication, authorization, and accounting into a single transaction. Instead, each function occurs independently, allowing network administrators to design highly granular access policies tailored to the needs of specific users and roles. For example, one TACACS+ session might include a dedicated authentication exchange to verify a user's credentials, followed by a separate authorization transaction to determine which commands the user is permitted to execute, and a final accounting process to log all user activities for auditing purposes.

TACACS+ messages, or packets, adhere to a well-defined structure that facilitates efficient and secure communication. Each packet begins with a header that contains essential information such as the protocol version, message type, sequence number, and session ID. The header also includes flags to indicate whether the message requires encryption and whether it marks the beginning or end of a session. By incorporating a session ID, TACACS+ ensures that all messages exchanged during a given session can be uniquely identified and correlated, even when multiple sessions are active concurrently between the same client and server.

The payload of a TACACS+ packet contains the actual data relevant to the AAA process being conducted. Depending on the type of message—whether it is an authentication request, an authorization response, or an accounting record—the payload may include a variety of fields such as the username, password, requested service, command strings, privilege levels, and accounting attributes. TACACS+ supports a variety of authentication methods, including ASCII, PAP, CHAP, and MS-CHAP, providing flexibility to integrate with different network and security environments. All of these payload elements can be fully encrypted, a critical security feature that sets TACACS+ apart from protocols like RADIUS, which only encrypt the password during authentication.

Encryption within TACACS+ is implemented at the application layer, providing end-to-end protection for all session data. The protocol encrypts not just credentials but also the commands being issued by users and the detailed accounting records generated during a session. This level of encryption helps mitigate risks associated with packet sniffing, man-in-the-middle attacks, and other common threats that target network communication. The encryption keys used are derived from shared secrets configured on both the client and the server, ensuring that only trusted parties can decrypt and interpret the messages.

TACACS+ sessions follow a logical sequence of operations. A session typically starts when a user attempts to access a network device by logging in through a console, SSH, or Telnet session. The client device initiates an authentication request, forwarding the user's credentials to the TACACS+ server. Upon successful authentication, the client then issues an authorization request, detailing the specific service or command the user is attempting to execute. The server evaluates the request against its configured policies and returns an authorization response indicating whether the requested action is permitted, denied, or requires further interaction. If authorization is granted, the user may proceed, and any subsequent actions—such as additional commands—may trigger further authorization checks.

Accounting transactions can occur both during and after a session. For example, TACACS+ can be configured to log all commands executed by the user in real time, generating accounting records that are sent back to the server. These records include vital session information such as the start and end times, the commands executed, the outcomes of those commands, and other contextual data. These logs are invaluable for auditing, compliance, and forensic analysis, offering organizations a clear and traceable record of administrative activity on their network infrastructure.

Another notable aspect of TACACS+ protocol architecture is its extensibility. The protocol is designed to accommodate custom attributes and vendor-specific extensions, which makes it highly adaptable to specialized environments. This flexibility is particularly advantageous for large enterprises and service providers that require fine-tuned access control policies tailored to specific operational workflows or compliance frameworks. Vendors can develop custom command sets and privilege levels that integrate seamlessly with TACACS+ transactions, further enhancing its utility.

The architecture of TACACS+ also facilitates centralized control and simplified administration. By consolidating user account management and access policies on a single TACACS+ server or server cluster, organizations reduce administrative overhead and minimize the likelihood of misconfigurations. Changes to user roles, permissions, or authentication methods can be applied universally across the network from a single point, eliminating the need for repetitive, manual updates to individual devices. This centralized model not only streamlines operations but also strengthens security by ensuring consistent enforcement of access control policies.

In large-scale or mission-critical networks, the TACACS+ architecture supports redundancy and load balancing to ensure high availability. Organizations can deploy multiple TACACS+ servers in an active-active or active-passive configuration, allowing client devices to fail over automatically if the primary server becomes unreachable. This design mitigates the risk of service outages and ensures that critical network infrastructure remains protected and operational even during server maintenance or network disruptions.

TACACS+ protocol architecture exemplifies a balance between security, flexibility, and manageability. It is designed to address the diverse needs of modern organizations, from securing administrative access to network devices to providing detailed, auditable records of user activity. By adopting a modular and extensible approach, TACACS+ has established itself as a foundational component of network security strategies, capable of supporting complex environments with evolving security and operational requirements.

Understanding the AAA Framework

The AAA framework, which stands for Authentication, Authorization, and Accounting, is a fundamental concept in network security and access management. It provides a structured approach to controlling and monitoring access to network resources, ensuring that only authorized users can interact with systems, and that their activities are tracked for accountability and security purposes. In modern networking, the AAA model is implemented through various protocols and technologies, with TACACS+ and RADIUS being among the most common. However, the framework itself transcends specific implementations, serving as a blueprint for building robust and scalable access control systems across diverse network environments.

Authentication is the first pillar of the AAA framework and acts as the initial barrier to network access. Its primary role is to verify the identity of a user, device, or system attempting to connect to a network resource. Authentication is essential in preventing unauthorized entities from gaining entry to sensitive systems or data. The process typically involves presenting credentials, such as a username and password, security token, digital certificate, or biometric data, which are then validated against a trusted repository. This repository may be a local database, an LDAP directory, or a third-party identity provider. In some cases, multi-factor authentication is implemented, requiring users to present multiple forms of evidence to prove their identity, thus significantly strengthening the security posture. Without effective authentication mechanisms, networks would be vulnerable to a wide range of attacks, including credential stuffing, brute force attacks, and unauthorized access attempts.

Once a user's identity has been successfully authenticated, the next phase is authorization. Authorization determines what actions the authenticated user is permitted to perform and what resources they are allowed to access. This step enforces the principle of least privilege, a core security concept where users are granted the minimum level of access necessary to perform their duties. In practice, authorization policies can range from broad permissions, such as granting full administrative rights to network devices, to highly specific controls, such as allowing a user to execute only a limited set of commands on a router. Authorization decisions are often based on user roles, security group memberships, or predefined access control lists. In the AAA framework, authorization ensures that even legitimate users cannot overstep their intended boundaries, reducing the likelihood of both accidental misconfigurations and deliberate misuse of network resources.

Accounting, the final component of the AAA framework, involves the collection and storage of information related to user activities within the network. This data serves multiple purposes, including auditing, compliance, capacity planning, and forensic analysis. Accounting logs typically capture details such as login times, logout times, commands executed, data accessed, and any system modifications performed during a user session. These records are vital for organizations to detect anomalies, investigate incidents, and maintain transparency in network operations. Accounting also plays a crucial role in regulatory compliance, as many industry standards and legal frameworks require organizations to maintain detailed logs of user activities to ensure accountability and traceability.

The AAA framework operates as a continuous cycle, where each component feeds into and reinforces the others. Authentication gates access to the network, authorization governs actions once inside, and accounting provides a comprehensive audit trail. The seamless integration of these three functions forms a security architecture that is both proactive and reactive. It proactively prevents unauthorized access and enforces policy-based controls, while also providing reactive capabilities by capturing detailed logs that can be analyzed when incidents occur.

In a networked environment, AAA is typically implemented using dedicated servers, often referred to as AAA servers, which handle all authentication, authorization, and accounting requests from network devices acting as clients. These servers centralize access control decisions and provide consistency across the network, eliminating the need to manage access policies individually on each device. Protocols such as TACACS+ and RADIUS facilitate this interaction between clients and servers, with each protocol delivering AAA services in slightly different ways depending on the organization's operational and security requirements.

AAA is not limited to network devices alone. It is widely used across multiple layers of an IT ecosystem, including virtual private networks, wireless access points, firewalls, web applications, and cloud services. For example, when a remote user attempts to establish a VPN connection, the AAA server will authenticate the user, determine what internal resources the user can access based on authorization rules, and log the entire session through accounting mechanisms. This ensures that even in complex, multi-cloud or hybrid environments, consistent and enforceable access control policies can be applied across a wide range of platforms and services.

As organizations continue to grow and adopt digital transformation initiatives, the AAA framework has expanded to support emerging technologies such as identity federation, single sign-on (SSO), and zero trust architecture. Identity federation enables users to access multiple systems or services across different organizational boundaries using a single set of credentials. SSO simplifies the user experience by allowing users to authenticate once and gain access to multiple applications without re-entering credentials, while still maintaining strong security controls based on AAA principles. Zero trust architecture takes the concept even further by removing implicit trust from the network perimeter and requiring continuous authentication and authorization for every access request, no matter where it originates.

In highly regulated industries such as finance, healthcare, and critical infrastructure, the importance of AAA cannot be overstated. Regulatory bodies mandate strict controls over access to sensitive systems and data, and failure to implement adequate AAA measures can result in legal penalties, reputational damage, and significant financial losses. The detailed accounting records generated by the AAA framework serve as evidence of compliance with regulatory standards such as GDPR, HIPAA, PCI DSS, and ISO 27001.

The flexibility of the AAA model allows it to be adapted to various deployment scenarios. It can be integrated into legacy systems or extended to cloud-native environments with ease. For instance, modern identity-as-a-service (IDaaS) platforms build upon the AAA framework to provide centralized identity management and access control across distributed cloud applications. This adaptability ensures that the AAA model remains relevant and effective in the face of evolving technological landscapes and security challenges.

Ultimately, the AAA framework provides the backbone for network security and user accountability. It is an essential component in safeguarding organizational assets, preventing data breaches, and ensuring operational integrity. The effectiveness of any access control solution relies heavily on how well it implements the AAA model and how thoroughly organizations integrate these principles into their security policies and daily operations. By maintaining a clear focus on authentication, authorization, and accounting, organizations can create secure and resilient network infrastructures capable of supporting modern business requirements.

Deep Dive into Authentication Processes

Authentication is one of the most critical components of network security, serving as the foundation upon which secure access to systems and resources is built. It is the process through which a system verifies the identity of a user, device, or entity requesting access to protected resources. This verification process helps ensure that only legitimate users can access sensitive data, critical systems, or perform specific actions within a network environment. As cyber threats have evolved in sophistication and frequency, the importance of a robust and flexible authentication process has become paramount for organizations of all sizes and industries.

At its core, the authentication process starts when a user attempts to gain access to a system, network device, or service. The user must present credentials to prove their identity. Traditionally, this has involved the use of a simple username and password combination. However, the reliance on passwords alone has proven to be a significant vulnerability, as passwords can be guessed, stolen, or cracked through brute force attacks. To address these risks, modern authentication processes have moved towards more complex methods, incorporating multiple factors and layers of verification.

The most widely known approach to strengthening authentication is multi-factor authentication, which requires users to present two or more pieces of evidence to prove their identity. These factors generally fall into three categories: something the user knows, such as a password or PIN; something the user has, such as a smart card, hardware token, or mobile authenticator; and something the user is, referring to biometric attributes like fingerprints, facial recognition, or retina scans. By requiring multiple types of factors, organizations significantly reduce the likelihood of unauthorized access, even if one of the factors, like a password, is compromised.

In the context of network infrastructure, authentication processes are frequently handled by AAA protocols such as TACACS+ and RADIUS. When a user attempts to access a network device like a router or switch, the device acts as a client, forwarding the user's credentials to a centralized AAA server. The server then compares these credentials against a user database, which may be stored locally or integrated with external identity management systems such as LDAP, Active Directory, or cloud-based identity providers. If the provided credentials match the stored records and meet the system's authentication policies, the user is authenticated and allowed to proceed to the next phase of the AAA process.

Authentication mechanisms can vary depending on the organization's security requirements and the sensitivity of the resources being accessed. For low-risk systems, simple password-based authentication may still be used, though it is typically augmented with additional controls such as password complexity rules, expiration policies, and account lockout thresholds to reduce vulnerability to attacks. For more critical systems, stronger methods like certificate-based authentication or token-based authentication are preferred. In certificate-based authentication, digital certificates issued by a trusted Certificate Authority are used to verify a user's or device's identity, enabling secure, cryptographic validation without transmitting passwords over the network.

An increasingly common method used in modern authentication workflows is challenge-response authentication. This technique enhances security by ensuring that no passwords are transmitted in plaintext across the network. Instead, when a user initiates an authentication request, the server issues a challenge, often a random string of data. The user's system then applies a cryptographic hash or encryption function to the challenge combined with their secret (such as a password or private key) and returns the response to the server. The server performs the same computation and compares the results. If the values match, authentication is successful. Variants of this approach are implemented in protocols like CHAP and MS-CHAP, which are supported by TACACS+ and RADIUS.

The move towards federated identity systems and single sign-on has further shaped the authentication landscape. In federated identity, users can authenticate with a central identity provider and access multiple, separate systems without needing to re-authenticate for each one. This model streamlines the user experience while maintaining strong authentication controls. Single sign-on extends this convenience within organizations, allowing employees to use a single set of credentials to access a variety of services, such as email, internal applications, and cloud-based tools, without needing to repeatedly enter passwords. Both of these models still rely on the integrity and security of the initial authentication process, underscoring the importance of robust credential management and session security.

Authentication is not a one-time event but often part of a continuous process. In modern zero trust architectures, authentication can be adaptive or dynamic, responding to changes in user behavior, device posture, or network context. For example, if a user typically logs in from a corporate network but suddenly attempts to access resources from a foreign IP address or an untrusted device, the system may require additional verification steps, such as answering security questions or completing a secondary factor challenge. This context-aware authentication process allows organizations to strike a balance between user convenience and security.

TACACS+ plays a pivotal role in authentication within network environments by facilitating secure, centralized verification of administrative users who need to configure or manage network devices. TACACS+ encrypts the entire payload of its authentication messages, including usernames, passwords, and session parameters, ensuring that sensitive information is protected from interception or tampering during transmission. This full encryption model is a key advantage over other protocols that may only encrypt specific fields. In critical infrastructure environments where the risk of cyberattack is high, this additional security is vital for safeguarding device management interfaces.

The authentication process also feeds into the broader auditing and compliance ecosystem. Every successful or failed authentication attempt generates logs that are collected by the AAA server and potentially forwarded to security information and event management systems for correlation and analysis. These logs provide critical insights into potential brute force attacks, compromised accounts, or insider threats, enabling security teams to respond to incidents quickly and effectively.

As technology continues to advance, so too does the field of authentication. Emerging methods such as passwordless authentication are gaining traction, leveraging technologies like public key infrastructure, biometric factors, and secure enclaves built into devices. These approaches aim to eliminate the need for traditional passwords altogether, reducing the attack surface and mitigating the risk of credential theft. However, even as new techniques emerge, the core principles of authentication remain consistent: verify identity with certainty, minimize the risk of unauthorized access, and integrate seamlessly into the larger security architecture.

Authentication processes are the gateway to any protected system or resource. Without a well-designed and effectively implemented authentication mechanism, even the most advanced network or application is vulnerable to compromise. It is the critical first step that enables organizations to enforce security policies, ensure regulatory compliance, and protect the integrity of their infrastructure in an increasingly complex and hostile digital landscape.

Authorization Mechanisms with TACACS+

Authorization is a key component of access control that dictates what authenticated users are allowed to do within a network. While authentication verifies who a user is, authorization defines what actions that user can perform and which resources they can access. In the context of TACACS+, authorization mechanisms are designed to provide fine-grained control over user privileges, especially in environments where administrative access to critical infrastructure devices needs to be tightly controlled. TACACS+ stands out for its ability to separate authorization from authentication and accounting, offering greater flexibility compared to other AAA protocols.

The authorization process in TACACS+ is initiated after successful user authentication. Once the user's identity is confirmed, the client device, such as a router or switch, sends an authorization request to the

TACACS+ server. This request contains details such as the user's identity, the requested service or command, the device's IP address, and other session-specific information. The TACACS+ server then evaluates this data against its configured policies to determine if the requested action should be permitted, denied, or restricted in some way. This decision is based on rules defined by network administrators, which are typically tailored to specific roles or job functions within the organization.

TACACS+ allows for highly detailed, command-level authorization. This means that administrators can create policies that grant or deny access to specific commands on network devices, rather than applying broad, general permissions. For example, an engineer might be allowed to view device configurations but prohibited from making changes, while a senior administrator may have full access to modify or reload a device. Command-level authorization provides a vital safeguard against unauthorized or accidental configuration changes, which could have serious consequences for network stability and security. This level of control is particularly valuable in large enterprises, service providers, and critical infrastructure networks where multiple teams with different responsibilities access the same devices.

The flexibility of TACACS+ authorization extends to the ability to define per-session attributes. Administrators can configure access control policies that adjust based on the time of day, the user's IP address, the device they are connecting to, or other contextual factors. For instance, a technician may only be allowed to perform certain maintenance tasks during a designated maintenance window, or a remote user might be limited to a specific set of commands to mitigate security risks. These dynamic policies give organizations the ability to enforce the principle of least privilege, ensuring that users have only the permissions they need at any given time.

TACACS+ also supports privilege levels, which are numeric values that represent different tiers of access within a network device. Privilege levels can be mapped to specific command sets, creating a hierarchy of permissions from read-only access to full administrative control. When a user initiates a session on a network device, the TACACS+ server returns an authorization response that includes the appropriate privilege level based on the user's identity and role. The device then enforces this privilege level, restricting or granting access to commands accordingly. This mechanism simplifies access management by grouping users into categories with predefined rights, streamlining policy enforcement while maintaining tight security controls.

One of the key benefits of TACACS+ authorization is that it centralizes policy management. Rather than configuring permissions individually on each device, administrators can define all access control rules on the TACACS+ server. This centralized approach ensures consistency across the entire network infrastructure and reduces the likelihood of configuration drift, where individual devices may have differing or outdated access policies. It also simplifies the process of onboarding new users or adjusting permissions for existing users, as changes only need to be made once on the TACACS+ server to take effect network-wide.

In addition to static policies, TACACS+ supports the use of attribute-value pairs (AVPs) in authorization responses. These AVPs provide additional instructions to the client device about how to handle the session. For example, an AVP might specify which virtual LAN (VLAN) a user should be placed into upon authentication or define session timeout values. In scenarios where TACACS+ is integrated with other security tools, such as Network Access Control (NAC) systems or identity management platforms, AVPs can also be used to enforce posture-based policies, restricting access based on the health or security posture of the connecting device.

TACACS+ authorization mechanisms are essential for meeting regulatory and compliance requirements. Industry standards such as PCI DSS, HIPAA, and ISO 27001 mandate strict controls over administrative access to critical systems and require organizations to demonstrate that only authorized personnel can perform sensitive actions. By providing granular control over who can do what on network devices, TACACS+ helps organizations meet these requirements and produce the necessary audit trails to prove compliance during assessments or investigations.

The separation of authorization from authentication also allows for better integration with external identity and access management

(IAM) systems. TACACS+ servers can work alongside directory services like LDAP or Active Directory, using the user's role or group membership information to dynamically assign permissions. This capability streamlines access control processes by aligning network device permissions with broader organizational identity policies, reducing administrative overhead and minimizing the risk of human error.

Authorization policies in TACACS+ can also be adapted to specific use cases. In service provider environments, for example, where engineers may manage equipment across multiple customer networks, TACACS+ can enforce customer-specific access controls that limit each engineer to their assigned customer infrastructure. In enterprise environments, TACACS+ authorization rules might enforce separation of duties, preventing users from combining sensitive actions, such as making a configuration change and disabling logging on the same device.

The real-time nature of TACACS+ authorization enhances operational security. Each time a user attempts to execute a privileged command, the client device consults the TACACS+ server to determine whether the action is allowed. This continuous interaction enables administrators to implement flexible and adaptive security policies, such as revoking certain permissions temporarily or applying additional scrutiny to commands issued from high-risk locations or untrusted devices.

The detailed logging generated by TACACS+ during the authorization process also contributes to an organization's overall security posture. Every authorization decision—whether it results in approval or denial—is logged and can be reviewed later for auditing purposes. These logs provide insight into user behavior, help detect patterns of misuse or policy violations, and serve as critical evidence in the event of a security incident. By correlating authorization logs with authentication and accounting records, security teams gain a comprehensive view of who accessed what systems, when, and how they interacted with those systems.

TACACS+ authorization mechanisms empower organizations to enforce strict access controls while maintaining operational efficiency. The protocol's ability to deliver granular, context-aware, and centralized authorization policies makes it a valuable tool in protecting modern network infrastructures from internal and external threats. By giving administrators precise control over network device interactions, TACACS+ strengthens security, supports compliance, and ensures that critical systems remain both secure and manageable.

Accounting and Auditing with TACACS+

Accounting and auditing are integral components of network security, providing the visibility and traceability necessary to maintain control over user activities and ensure regulatory compliance. Within the TACACS+ protocol, accounting serves as the mechanism for collecting detailed records of user actions on network devices, while auditing refers to the analysis of these records to detect anomalies, enforce policy adherence, and investigate security incidents. Together, accounting and auditing with TACACS+ play a pivotal role in strengthening the security posture of an organization by ensuring that every interaction with critical network infrastructure is recorded, reviewed, and verifiable.

The accounting process in TACACS+ begins once a user initiates an authenticated session on a network device such as a router, switch, firewall, or wireless controller. TACACS+ accounting records capture a wide range of session-related data, which includes but is not limited to login and logout times, session durations, executed commands, privilege levels, and the IP addresses of both the user and the device. This data is then transmitted from the network device, acting as a TACACS+ client, to the TACACS+ server, where it is stored securely for future analysis. These records provide a chronological log of user behavior, offering valuable insights into how the network is being accessed and managed on a daily basis.

TACACS+ supports different types of accounting records, including start, stop, and interim update records. A start record is generated when a user successfully authenticates and initiates a session. This record contains initial session data, such as the user's identity, the service or protocol used (such as SSH, Telnet, or console access), and the originating IP address. A stop record is created when the session ends, logging details such as the session's duration and the reason for termination, whether it was user-initiated, timed out, or forcibly closed by an administrator. Interim update records can be configured to provide periodic updates about an active session, allowing administrators to track ongoing activity and monitor session health in near real-time.

One of the most powerful features of TACACS+ accounting is command accounting, which provides granular visibility into every command executed by a user on a network device. For each command, the accounting system records details such as the timestamp, the exact command string, the privilege level at which the command was issued, and whether the command was successfully executed or generated an error. This level of detail is indispensable for auditing purposes, as it enables organizations to reconstruct user sessions, validate that configurations were performed according to policy, and identify potentially malicious or unauthorized activities.

The centralized nature of TACACS+ accounting enhances both operational efficiency and security. By collecting all accounting records in a single repository, organizations can implement standardized retention policies, enforce access controls on sensitive log data, and integrate accounting logs into broader security and compliance workflows. These centralized logs can be fed into security information and event management systems, or SIEMs, where they are correlated with other security data to detect patterns, generate alerts, and support incident response efforts. For example, if an administrator executes a series of high-privilege commands outside of normal working hours, this could trigger an automatic alert to the security operations team for immediate review.

Auditing with TACACS+ accounting data goes beyond reactive incident investigations. It is also a proactive measure that helps organizations identify gaps in their access control policies, verify the effectiveness of existing security controls, and ensure that users adhere to operational procedures. By regularly reviewing TACACS+ accounting logs, network administrators and security auditors can detect unusual activity patterns such as repeated failed login attempts, privilege escalations, or the execution of commands that deviate from normal operational baselines. These findings can then be used to refine access policies, strengthen authentication requirements, and mitigate potential security risks before they escalate into full-fledged incidents.

The role of TACACS+ in supporting regulatory compliance is equally significant. Many industries are subject to strict regulatory frameworks that mandate detailed logging and auditing of administrative access to critical systems. Standards such as PCI DSS, HIPAA, NIST, and ISO 27001 require organizations to demonstrate that only authorized personnel can access sensitive systems and that their activities are thoroughly documented. TACACS+ accounting provides the evidence needed to meet these requirements, offering a complete audit trail that can be presented during compliance audits or legal investigations. By showing that every administrative session and command has been logged, organizations can prove that they are adhering to industry best practices for security and accountability.

In complex network environments with multiple administrators or third-party vendors, TACACS+ accounting is vital for establishing accountability. When multiple users share responsibility for managing infrastructure devices, it becomes essential to track which individual performed specific actions. TACACS+ eliminates the risks associated with shared or generic accounts by enforcing individual user logins and creating distinct audit trails for each user. This ensures that all actions can be attributed to a specific person, reducing ambiguity and supporting the enforcement of separation of duties and least privilege principles.

Organizations can also leverage TACACS+ accounting data to enhance operational troubleshooting and performance monitoring. For example, when network outages or service degradations occur, reviewing TACACS+ logs can reveal if recent configuration changes or administrative actions contributed to the issue. By correlating timestamps from accounting records with system logs and network monitoring tools, engineers can pinpoint the root cause of problems more quickly and take corrective action. This improves network resilience and minimizes downtime by ensuring that administrators have access to accurate and comprehensive historical data.

TACACS+ accounting can be customized to suit the needs of different environments. Administrators can define which actions and events should trigger accounting records based on specific services, device types, or privilege levels. For example, accounting can be configured to log all activities on core network infrastructure while applying lighter logging policies to less critical systems. This level of customization helps balance the need for detailed auditing with storage and processing considerations, ensuring that log data remains both manageable and actionable.

TACACS+ accounting and auditing processes are integral to maintaining a secure and well-governed network environment. By capturing detailed records of user activity, providing visibility into administrative actions, and supporting forensic investigations, TACACS+ helps organizations reduce risk, enforce compliance, and strengthen trust in their network operations. The combination of detailed command logging, centralized log management, and seamless integration with broader security and auditing ecosystems makes TACACS+ an essential tool for any organization seeking to build a comprehensive access control and accountability framework.

Packet Structure and Data Flow in TACACS+

The packet structure and data flow of TACACS+ are fundamental aspects that define how the protocol operates, ensuring the secure and reliable exchange of AAA information between clients and servers. TACACS+ is a connection-oriented protocol that uses TCP as its transport mechanism, typically over port 49. The choice of TCP allows TACACS+ to benefit from TCP's inherent reliability features, such as error detection, retransmission, and flow control. This makes TACACS+ communications more resilient against packet loss or reordering issues that could otherwise affect the integrity of AAA transactions.

A TACACS+ packet is divided into two main sections: the header and the body. The header is a fixed-length structure that provides essential information about the packet, while the body contains variable-length data related to authentication, authorization, or accounting. Each packet sent between the TACACS+ client and server is carefully formatted to conform to these structural elements, allowing both parties to correctly parse and process the data.

The header of a TACACS+ packet consists of several key fields. These include the version number, which identifies the TACACS+ protocol version being used; the packet type, which indicates whether the packet is for authentication, authorization, accounting, or a response; and the sequence number, which helps ensure that packets are processed in the correct order. Additionally, the header contains a session ID, a unique identifier for each transaction session, ensuring that related packets are correctly associated with one another. The header also includes a flag that signals whether the body of the packet is encrypted, and a length field specifying the size of the packet body. These header fields play a crucial role in the integrity and confidentiality of TACACS+ communications.

The body of the TACACS+ packet varies depending on the type of AAA transaction. In an authentication request, the body might include the username, authentication method, service requested (such as login or command execution), and additional data such as a password or challenge-response token. For authorization requests, the body can contain information about the requested command, privilege level, and other context-specific details needed to determine whether the action should be permitted. Accounting packets, on the other hand, typically include session start and stop data, command logs, timestamps, and session outcome information. All of these elements are structured using a series of type-length-value (TLV) fields, providing a flexible way to encode a wide range of information without rigid constraints on field lengths.

A distinctive feature of TACACS+ packet structure is its approach to encryption. Unlike protocols such as RADIUS, which only encrypt the password field within authentication packets, TACACS+ encrypts the entire body of each packet. This full-payload encryption ensures that all transmitted data, including usernames, privilege levels, and accounting records, is protected from interception and tampering during transmission. The encryption key is derived from a shared secret configured on both the TACACS+ client and server, and this secret must be identical on both sides to allow successful decryption and verification of messages.

The data flow in a TACACS+ session follows a systematic process, beginning with the establishment of a TCP connection between the client, such as a network device, and the TACACS+ server. Once the connection is established, the client initiates an authentication request by sending a properly formatted TACACS+ packet containing the relevant user credentials and session parameters. The server processes this packet, decrypts the body if necessary, and validates the user's identity against its configured database or external directory services. The server then replies with an authentication response packet, indicating success, failure, or a need for further interaction, such as a challenge-response exchange.

If authentication is successful, the client proceeds by sending an authorization request packet. This packet contains details about the service or command the user is attempting to execute, along with session-specific information like privilege levels or device context. The TACACS+ server evaluates this data against its authorization policies and sends back an authorization response packet. This response may grant full permission, deny access, or return a set of additional parameters defining session restrictions, such as time limits or command limitations.

Once authorization is complete, accounting processes begin. The client generates accounting start packets at the beginning of the session, interim update packets during the session if configured to do so, and stop packets at the end of the session. These packets include detailed records about session activities and are sent to the TACACS+ server for logging and analysis. This ensures a comprehensive audit trail that tracks every significant action taken by the user, providing valuable data for both security and operational purposes.

Throughout the session, TACACS+ relies on its sequence numbering mechanism to maintain the order of packets. Each packet exchanged during a session increments the sequence number, helping prevent replay attacks and ensuring that both the client and server maintain synchronized transaction states. If packets arrive out of sequence or if sequence numbers do not match expected values, the session may be terminated or require re-initiation to maintain protocol integrity.

The communication model of TACACS+ is inherently request-response based, with each client-initiated request requiring a corresponding response from the server. This structure allows TACACS+ to maintain clear and predictable data flows that are easy to monitor and troubleshoot. Administrators can examine the flow of packets using debug tools on network devices and TACACS+ servers to diagnose authentication failures, authorization denials, or accounting discrepancies.

The efficiency of the TACACS+ packet structure and data flow also allows the protocol to scale in large environments with numerous simultaneous AAA transactions. By utilizing TCP's connection-oriented model and maintaining lightweight yet secure packet structures, TACACS+ minimizes overhead while ensuring reliable delivery and processing of AAA data. The protocol's ability to encapsulate complex, multi-step transactions into a series of structured packets makes it well-suited for both enterprise and service provider networks where control and visibility over administrative actions are essential.

The detailed and secure nature of TACACS+ packet structure and data flow helps organizations achieve a high degree of control over network access management. Every field, header element, and encrypted payload works in concert to create a robust and resilient system that can adapt to the varying security demands of different operational environments. The end-to-end encryption, combined with structured sequencing and transaction tracking, ensures that AAA data is handled with the integrity and confidentiality required in today's threat landscape. TACACS+ continues to serve as a foundational protocol for secure network access control, and its packet architecture remains one of its strongest technical advantages.

Encryption Techniques in TACACS+

Encryption is a cornerstone of TACACS+, serving as a critical mechanism for protecting the confidentiality and integrity of sensitive information transmitted between network devices and the TACACS+ server. In the modern threat landscape, where data interception and manipulation are common tactics used by attackers, the encryption techniques embedded in the TACACS+ protocol stand as a vital defense. Unlike other AAA protocols such as RADIUS, which only encrypt the password portion of its authentication packets, TACACS+ encrypts the entire body of every packet. This full-payload encryption provides a significant security advantage by ensuring that user credentials, authorization parameters, command requests, and accounting records are all shielded from potential eavesdroppers.

TACACS+ encryption operates at the application layer, offering end-to-end protection of data traveling over the TCP connection between the client and the server. The encryption is performed using a shared secret key, which must be pre-configured and identical on both the TACACS+ client and server for successful communication. This shared secret functions as the foundation for encrypting and decrypting packet payloads, ensuring that only trusted devices with the correct key can participate in TACACS+ transactions. The shared secret is never transmitted across the network, which further enhances the security of the key exchange process.

The encryption algorithm used by TACACS+ is typically a variant of the MD5 hashing function, which generates a unique hash value based on the shared secret, the session ID, and other dynamic values from the packet header. This hash is then applied to the body of the packet to encrypt the contents before transmission. The TACACS+ server performs the reverse process, using the same inputs to generate the corresponding hash and decrypt the payload for processing. Although MD5 is widely considered obsolete for cryptographic applications due to vulnerabilities to collision attacks, within TACACS+, it is used in a controlled context as a message digest rather than for storing or protecting long-term secrets.

The key aspect of TACACS+ encryption lies in its ability to safeguard the entire transaction payload. By encrypting every byte of data within the packet body, TACACS+ ensures that critical information such as usernames, command strings, session parameters, and accounting details remain concealed from network sniffers or attackers performing man-in-the-middle attacks. This protection is especially valuable when TACACS+ is used to manage administrative access to core network devices, where intercepted commands or session data could provide attackers with a blueprint of the organization's infrastructure or expose weaknesses that could be exploited.

Encryption within TACACS+ is applied on a per-packet basis, meaning that each individual packet sent during an AAA transaction undergoes the encryption process independently. This packet-level encryption model provides an additional layer of security because even if an attacker were to capture multiple packets, decrypting one packet would not reveal the contents of others. Each packet relies on unique session information, such as the session ID and sequence number, to contribute to the hash calculation, effectively preventing replay attacks or the reassembly of complete transaction flows from intercepted fragments.

In addition to encryption, TACACS+ incorporates integrity checking mechanisms to verify that the payload has not been altered during transit. The decryption process inherently checks the validity of the payload, as any mismatch in the shared secret or tampering with the packet data would result in a failed decryption. This ensures that TACACS+ not only protects the confidentiality of the data but also maintains its integrity by preventing unauthorized modification of session information, user commands, or accounting records.

TACACS+ encryption techniques are well suited for protecting highly sensitive environments, such as enterprise networks, government agencies, financial institutions, and service providers. In these settings, the threat of interception is elevated due to the value of the data being transmitted and the critical nature of the infrastructure being managed. TACACS+ encryption helps mitigate this risk by eliminating the exposure of clear-text administrative commands and session logs, reducing the attack surface available to malicious actors who may be monitoring network traffic.

While the built-in encryption model of TACACS+ provides strong protection on its own, organizations often deploy additional security measures to enhance communication security further. TACACS+ traffic is frequently encapsulated within secure tunnels such as IPsec VPNs or SSL/TLS-based transport tunnels. This layered security approach, commonly referred to as defense in depth, ensures that even if one layer of encryption is compromised, the data remains protected by subsequent layers. For example, encrypting TACACS+ traffic within an IPsec tunnel provides protection at the network layer, safeguarding not only the TACACS+ payloads but also the packet headers and session metadata.

The decision to implement TACACS+ with or without additional tunnel encryption is often based on an organization's security policy and threat model. In highly segmented or sensitive networks, where strict compliance and regulatory requirements apply, using both TACACS+ native encryption and external tunneling mechanisms is considered a best practice. In contrast, in trusted internal networks with limited external exposure, organizations may rely on TACACS+ encryption alone to meet operational needs while maintaining network performance.

Encryption within TACACS+ also enables organizations to enforce security uniformly across diverse network devices and platforms. TACACS+ is designed to be vendor-agnostic, meaning that it can be integrated into equipment from multiple manufacturers while still providing the same level of encryption and security. This interoperability allows organizations to standardize AAA services while maintaining strong encryption controls, regardless of the underlying hardware or software differences among network devices.

Another advantage of the TACACS+ encryption model is its minimal impact on performance. The application-layer encryption and decryption processes are lightweight enough to operate efficiently on both client devices and TACACS+ servers, even in high-traffic environments. Modern network devices and servers are equipped with sufficient processing capabilities to handle encryption overhead without noticeable degradation in transaction speed or latency. This ensures that security does not come at the expense of network responsiveness, which is critical in large-scale networks where high volumes of AAA requests are processed continuously.

TACACS+ encryption techniques provide a well-balanced approach to securing AAA data by combining robust payload protection, flexible deployment options, and compatibility with external security measures. By encrypting the full packet body, TACACS+ ensures that sensitive information related to authentication, authorization, and accounting is safeguarded from prying eyes throughout its journey across the network. This commitment to security has established TACACS+ as a preferred choice for organizations seeking to implement reliable and comprehensive access control protocols in environments where protecting administrative access and operational data is a top priority.

Setting Up a TACACS+ Server

Setting up a TACACS+ server is a crucial step in implementing centralized access control within an organization's network infrastructure. The server acts as the central point for handling authentication, authorization, and accounting requests coming from multiple network devices. By configuring a TACACS+ server, administrators can ensure consistent access policies, simplify user management, and enhance security across routers, switches, firewalls, and other critical devices. The process begins with selecting the appropriate software to function as the TACACS+ server, followed by installing and configuring the service to meet the specific needs of the organization's network environment.

A common choice for a TACACS+ server is an open-source implementation such as tac_plus, which is widely used due to its flexibility and support for various network environments. Alternatively, some organizations may opt for commercial TACACS+ solutions integrated into broader network access control or identity management platforms. Regardless of the implementation, the server requires a reliable host system, typically a Linux-based server or a hardened appliance, to ensure availability and performance under operational loads.

Once the server operating system is prepared and updated with the latest security patches, the next step is to install the TACACS+ daemon. In the case of tac_plus, this often involves downloading the source code or using a package manager depending on the Linux distribution. After the TACACS+ service is installed, attention shifts to configuring the core elements of the server, primarily through the tac_plus configuration file. This file governs how the server handles authentication, authorization, and accounting requests from client devices and specifies user accounts, access policies, encryption keys, and logging preferences.

A fundamental component of the configuration file is the definition of client devices. Each network device that will send AAA requests to the TACACS+ server must be defined with its corresponding IP address and a shared secret. The shared secret acts as a password known only to the client and the server, forming the basis for encrypting TACACS+ packets. This secret should be strong and unique to prevent unauthorized devices from attempting to communicate with the TACACS+ server. The configuration will specify the permitted IP addresses and the associated key for each client device, enabling the server to identify and securely interact with the defined clients.

User accounts and group definitions are equally critical when configuring a TACACS+ server. User definitions include specifying usernames, passwords, and access permissions. Passwords may be stored locally in the TACACS+ configuration file, but in many enterprise deployments, integration with external authentication systems such as LDAP, Active Directory, or RADIUS is preferred to streamline user management. User accounts can also be organized into groups to simplify authorization policies. For example, a group might be created for network administrators with full device privileges, while another group might be designated for operators with read-only access. Group assignments make it easier to manage permissions consistently across multiple users.

Authorization settings within the configuration file determine what services or commands users are allowed to access on the network devices. This level of control is what sets TACACS+ apart from other AAA protocols. The configuration can include command authorization policies that specify which commands are allowed, denied, or require additional approval before execution. These rules can be applied globally or tailored to specific users or groups, allowing for detailed customization of permissions based on job roles or operational needs.

Accounting configuration is another essential part of setting up the TACACS+ server. Administrators can enable accounting to record detailed logs of user activity, including session start and stop events, executed commands, and session durations. The accounting data can be written to local log files on the server or sent to a centralized logging system or SIEM platform for further analysis. Accurate accounting is crucial for auditing, compliance, and incident response, providing a comprehensive record of administrative actions taken on network devices.

Once the TACACS+ configuration is complete, the server must be started and monitored to ensure it is running correctly. Administrators typically launch the tac_plus daemon in the background and verify its status using system monitoring tools or built-in diagnostic commands. Debugging options can be enabled to produce verbose logs, which are helpful during the initial setup to confirm that the server is correctly processing requests and responding to client devices. These logs detail each step of the AAA process, from the initial authentication handshake to authorization decisions and accounting records, providing valuable insights for troubleshooting.

To finalize the TACACS+ server setup, network devices must be configured to communicate with the server. This involves specifying the TACACS+ server's IP address, the shared secret, and enabling TACACS+ as the AAA method on the device. On Cisco devices, for example, administrators use specific IOS commands to configure TACACS+ servers, set authentication priorities, and define fallback mechanisms in case the TACACS+ server is unreachable. Properly configuring both the server and client devices ensures smooth and secure operation of AAA services across the network.

Hardening the TACACS+ server is a vital final step before moving into production. This includes applying security best practices such as limiting access to the server through firewall rules, disabling unnecessary services, enforcing strong authentication policies for administrators managing the server, and regularly updating the system to patch vulnerabilities. Additionally, securing the communication channel with the TACACS+ server can be enhanced by placing the server behind a VPN or in a management VLAN isolated from general network traffic.

Scalability and high availability should also be considered when setting up the TACACS+ server. In large or mission-critical environments, deploying redundant TACACS+ servers configured in an active-passive or active-active model ensures continued AAA service availability if one server fails. Load balancing techniques may also be applied to distribute AAA request loads evenly across multiple servers, improving performance and reliability.

Setting up a TACACS+ server provides organizations with centralized control over who can access network infrastructure, what actions they can perform, and how those actions are monitored and logged. By configuring the server to meet operational and security requirements, network administrators create a framework that supports accountability, consistency, and security across the enterprise. The setup process is both technical and strategic, requiring careful planning to align with business needs while adhering to industry best practices for securing administrative access to critical systems.

Configuring TACACS+ Clients

Configuring TACACS+ clients is an essential step in deploying a centralized AAA solution within any network environment. The TACACS+ client refers to the network device that communicates directly with the TACACS+ server to request authentication, authorization, and accounting services. These clients are typically routers, switches, firewalls, wireless controllers, or any other devices where administrative access must be strictly controlled and logged. The goal of configuring TACACS+ clients is to ensure that these devices forward all AAA-related requests to the TACACS+ server, providing consistency in access control across the entire network infrastructure.

The configuration process begins by defining the TACACS+ server within the client device's operating system or configuration interface. On Cisco IOS devices, for example, this starts with specifying the IP address of the TACACS+ server and associating it with a shared secret. This shared secret is critical, as it is used to encrypt the communication between the client and the TACACS+ server. Both the client and the server must have identical shared secrets configured for secure and successful communication. A strong shared secret should include a combination of uppercase and lowercase letters, numbers, and special characters to reduce the risk of brute force attacks or unauthorized device pairing.

Once the TACACS+ server is defined, the next step is to configure the AAA model on the client device. This involves enabling the AAA feature globally and specifying TACACS+ as the preferred method for authentication, authorization, and accounting. Administrators must define AAA methods for each of these three components individually to ensure the device knows how to handle user logins, what permissions to apply, and how to log user activity. For instance, administrators can set TACACS+ as the primary method for login authentication, while also defining a fallback to local authentication in case the TACACS+ server becomes temporarily unavailable. This redundancy ensures that administrators can still access the device for critical operations even if the AAA server is unreachable due to network issues or maintenance.

With authentication configured, authorization settings are applied next. These settings instruct the client device to consult the TACACS+ server before allowing any administrative commands to be executed. Authorization can be configured to apply globally or to specific command sets depending on the privilege level of the user. This step ensures that even authenticated users are restricted to executing only the commands they are permitted to run based on policies defined centrally on the TACACS+ server. This provides a consistent security model across all network devices, enforcing least privilege and reducing the likelihood of accidental or malicious configuration changes.

The third component of the configuration process involves enabling accounting on the client device. Accounting ensures that every administrative action, including successful and failed login attempts, executed commands, and session start and stop events, is logged and sent to the TACACS+ server. This provides detailed records that can be used for compliance audits, security investigations, and operational analysis. The accounting configuration typically includes session accounting to track when users log in and log out, and command accounting to log every command entered during the session. Some organizations also configure interim accounting updates to provide real-time visibility into active sessions.

As part of the client configuration, it is also important to consider how authentication prompts will be handled. For example, on Cisco devices, administrators can customize login banners and authentication prompts to include security notices or compliance warnings. These small details reinforce security awareness among users and contribute to organizational compliance efforts.

When configuring TACACS+ clients in environments with multiple TACACS+ servers for redundancy, administrators define a list of servers with an order of preference. The client will attempt to contact the first server in the list and, if that server is unreachable, it will automatically fail over to the next available server. This high-availability configuration helps ensure uninterrupted AAA services, minimizing the risk of service disruption during server outages or maintenance windows.

Configuring TACACS+ clients also includes applying security best practices to further strengthen the overall AAA setup. Administrators should restrict access to the management plane of network devices by using access control lists (ACLs) to limit which IP addresses or networks can initiate TACACS+ sessions. For instance, only TACACS+ servers and authorized management stations should be allowed to access the device's administrative interfaces such as SSH, Telnet, or the web GUI. Disabling unused management protocols and restricting administrative access to secure protocols like SSH is also recommended to minimize the attack surface.

In addition to security measures, performance and usability considerations are also important when configuring TACACS+ clients. For example, setting appropriate timeout values and retry limits ensures that devices do not hang or cause delays if the TACACS+ server is slow to respond or temporarily unavailable. Administrators can define how many times a device should retry contacting the server before switching to the local fallback authentication method.

In multi-vendor environments where non-Cisco devices are also configured as TACACS+ clients, administrators may encounter slight differences in how each device implements TACACS+ support. However, the fundamental concepts remain the same: defining the TACACS+ server address and shared secret, enabling AAA, specifying

TACACS+ as the preferred method for authentication, authorization, and accounting, and configuring fallback mechanisms. Some platforms, such as Juniper, Arista, or Fortinet, may use different syntax or commands, but they still conform to the overall TACACS+ communication model.

After the basic client configuration is complete, it is critical to conduct extensive testing before deploying the changes to production. Administrators should verify that authentication requests are correctly forwarded to the TACACS+ server and that successful and failed login attempts are logged as expected. They should also validate that authorization policies are enforced, such as restricting command access based on user roles, and that accounting records are being generated and sent to the server in a timely manner.

A well-configured TACACS+ client helps to create a uniform, centralized access control model across the network, allowing security teams and administrators to enforce policies consistently, monitor user activity effectively, and respond quickly to potential incidents. By centralizing AAA functions through properly configured TACACS+ clients, organizations improve their operational efficiency, reduce administrative overhead, and enhance the overall security posture of their network infrastructure. The effort put into careful planning and configuration of each client device ensures that the full benefits of TACACS+ can be realized across diverse and complex network environments.

User Database Management

User database management is a crucial component in any TACACS+ deployment as it directly influences how users are authenticated, authorized, and accounted for across the network. The user database serves as the repository where user identities, passwords, group memberships, and access control policies are stored and managed. Whether configured locally on the TACACS+ server or integrated with external identity management systems, the database is at the core of how access control decisions are made, ensuring that only authorized personnel can interact with critical network resources.

The most basic form of user database management in TACACS+ involves maintaining a local database within the TACACS+ server's configuration files. In this model, user accounts are manually defined in the tac_plus configuration file, specifying usernames, passwords, and associated privileges. Each user entry typically includes fields such as the user's login name, password hash, assigned privilege level, and command authorization policies. While this method is straightforward and effective in small-scale environments, it requires manual updates for every addition, modification, or deletion of user accounts, which can become time-consuming and error-prone as the network scales.

To improve operational efficiency and centralize user management, many organizations integrate TACACS+ with external authentication services such as LDAP or Active Directory. This integration allows the TACACS+ server to act as a proxy, forwarding authentication requests to the external directory service while continuing to handle authorization and accounting functions internally. By doing so, administrators can manage user accounts centrally in a corporate directory, reducing redundancy and ensuring consistent identity management across various systems and services. For example, when integrated with Active Directory, any user modifications—such as password changes or role reassignments—are automatically reflected in TACACS+ authentication workflows without the need to manually edit the TACACS+ configuration file.

In environments where LDAP or Active Directory integration is not used, maintaining a local user database requires diligent administration. Passwords should be securely hashed using cryptographic functions, and strong password policies must be enforced to prevent weak or easily guessable credentials. The local database must also be reviewed regularly to ensure that accounts belonging to former employees, contractors, or temporary users are promptly deactivated or removed, reducing the risk of unauthorized access. User entries can be grouped into roles or user classes within the TACACS+ configuration file to streamline authorization management. Group-based policies enable administrators to assign permissions collectively, rather than on a per-user basis, making the user database easier to maintain and update.

In addition to account creation and password management, user database management also involves defining privilege levels. Privilege levels specify what actions a user is authorized to perform on a network device. Commonly, privilege levels are numeric values that correspond to specific permission sets. For example, a privilege level of 15 might grant full administrative rights, while lower levels may restrict the user to monitoring or diagnostic commands. By mapping users or groups to appropriate privilege levels, administrators can enforce the principle of least privilege, ensuring that users are only granted the minimum access necessary to perform their job functions.

Another key aspect of user database management in TACACS+ is the configuration of command authorization policies. These policies define which commands are permitted, denied, or require additional review for each user or group. In complex network environments where different teams manage different aspects of the infrastructure, command-level control is vital for preventing unauthorized or accidental changes. For instance, a network technician might be allowed to run diagnostic commands but prohibited from modifying routing tables or disabling security features. These policies are tightly coupled with the user database and must be carefully designed and tested to strike a balance between operational flexibility and security.

Scalability is a common challenge in managing user databases, especially as organizations grow and the number of devices and users increases. To address this, many organizations implement automated tools and scripts to help manage and synchronize user databases. Automation can assist with routine tasks such as adding new users, updating passwords, or assigning users to appropriate groups. For example, integration with configuration management tools like Ansible or Puppet can streamline the deployment of updated TACACS+ configuration files to multiple servers, ensuring consistency across distributed environments.

Auditing and logging are also essential elements tied to user database management. Every authentication and authorization attempt involving a user in the database is recorded as part of TACACS+ accounting logs. These logs provide valuable insights into user activity and are essential for compliance reporting, incident investigation, and operational analysis. Properly managing the user database ensures that audit trails are accurate, as they are directly linked to user identities defined within the system.

Organizations should also implement clear procedures for managing privileged accounts, sometimes referred to as superusers or administrators. These accounts often have unrestricted access to network devices and, as such, require additional oversight. Measures such as multi-factor authentication, session recording, and frequent privilege reviews should be applied to these high-risk accounts to reduce the chance of misuse or insider threats. Regular audits of privileged accounts should be performed to verify that access is still necessary and that permissions align with current job responsibilities.

Maintaining documentation is another best practice in user database management. Administrators should maintain a record of who has access to what systems, the roles and privileges assigned to each user, and the rationale for these assignments. Documentation helps ensure transparency, supports security audits, and facilitates knowledge transfer among team members responsible for managing the TACACS+ server and related infrastructure.

Finally, user database management should be guided by the organization's overall security policies and compliance requirements. Standards such as ISO 27001, NIST 800-53, PCI DSS, and HIPAA often dictate specific requirements for managing user accounts, including enforcing strong passwords, reviewing user access regularly, and maintaining audit trails of account activity. By aligning TACACS+ user database management practices with these standards, organizations can strengthen their security posture while demonstrating due diligence to regulatory bodies and stakeholders.

An efficiently managed user database is critical to the success of any TACACS+ deployment. Whether operating with a local user file or through integration with centralized identity management platforms, effective user database management supports secure, consistent, and scalable access control across the network. By focusing on user account accuracy, privilege enforcement, password security, and audit readiness, organizations can ensure that their TACACS+ environment remains a strong and reliable component of their broader security architecture.

Integrating TACACS+ with LDAP and Active Directory

Integrating TACACS+ with LDAP and Active Directory is a strategic approach that enhances centralized user management and streamlines authentication processes across an organization's network infrastructure. While TACACS+ is a robust protocol for handling authentication, authorization, and accounting, managing large numbers of user accounts directly in the TACACS+ server's local database can quickly become impractical in enterprise environments. By linking TACACS+ to LDAP or Active Directory services, organizations can achieve a seamless and scalable identity management framework that improves efficiency, consistency, and security.

LDAP, or Lightweight Directory Access Protocol, is an industry-standard protocol used to access and manage directory information over an IP network. Active Directory, Microsoft's directory service, is built on LDAP and adds additional features such as Group Policy and Kerberos-based authentication. Both LDAP and Active Directory are widely used as centralized repositories for storing user credentials, group memberships, and other identity-related attributes. Integrating TACACS+ with these directory services allows organizations to leverage existing user accounts and authentication policies without duplicating account information in multiple systems.

The integration process typically involves configuring the TACACS+ server to act as a gateway between the network devices and the LDAP or Active Directory service. When a network device acting as a TACACS+ client sends an authentication request to the TACACS+ server, the server forwards the authentication credentials to the directory service for verification. If the user is authenticated successfully in LDAP or Active Directory, the TACACS+ server then proceeds to handle the authorization and accounting steps based on its configured policies.

To begin integration, administrators must configure the TACACS+ server to communicate with the LDAP or Active Directory server. This is usually accomplished by editing the TACACS+ configuration file to specify LDAP or AD as the authentication backend. Parameters such as the directory server's IP address or hostname, the communication port (usually 389 for LDAP or 636 for LDAPS), and the distinguished name (DN) of the base search directory must be defined. Additionally, the TACACS+ server requires credentials to bind to the directory service, typically in the form of a service account with read permissions to user objects. For security purposes, communication between the TACACS+ server and the directory service should be encrypted using SSL/TLS to protect credentials and directory queries from interception.

The search filter is another important component of the integration. The filter defines the criteria the TACACS+ server will use to locate user records within the LDAP or Active Directory database. For instance, the filter might specify that user accounts must be located within a specific organizational unit (OU) or must belong to a particular security group. This filtering mechanism ensures that only valid users with the correct attributes are eligible for authentication via TACACS+, enhancing security and ensuring alignment with organizational policies.

Once a user is successfully authenticated via LDAP or Active Directory, TACACS+ continues the AAA workflow by applying authorization policies defined in its local configuration. These policies determine the user's privilege level, permissible commands, and access rights on network devices. While LDAP and Active Directory handle authentication, TACACS+ retains control over authorization and accounting, maintaining the protocol's signature granularity in defining access policies. This hybrid model enables organizations to centralize identity verification while preserving fine-grained control over user privileges on network infrastructure.

In addition to authentication, group memberships in Active Directory or LDAP can be leveraged to dynamically assign users to specific roles or access levels within TACACS+. For example, a user who belongs to an "Admin" group in Active Directory can be mapped to a higher privilege level in TACACS+, while a user from an "Operators" group may be assigned read-only access. This mapping allows administrators to maintain consistent role-based access control (RBAC) across both the directory service and the TACACS+ environment, reducing administrative overhead and minimizing the risk of misaligned permissions.

Integrating TACACS+ with LDAP or Active Directory also provides operational advantages in terms of user lifecycle management. When a user is added, modified, or removed in the directory service, these changes are automatically reflected in the TACACS+ authentication process without requiring manual updates to the TACACS+ server's local database. This synchronization streamlines user onboarding and offboarding processes, improves accuracy, and reduces the risk of orphaned accounts that could be exploited for unauthorized access.

For organizations operating in hybrid environments that include both Windows-based and non-Windows systems, integrating TACACS+ with Active Directory provides an additional benefit. Many network devices and Unix-based systems can authenticate against Active Directory via TACACS+, allowing for unified credential management across diverse platforms. This interoperability simplifies user management and strengthens security by enforcing the same password policies, account lockout thresholds, and authentication methods throughout the entire organization.

Security is a critical consideration in any integration involving user credentials. When configuring TACACS+ to query LDAP or Active Directory, it is essential to enforce secure transport methods, such as LDAPS or StartTLS, to protect the confidentiality of authentication requests and directory responses. The service account used for directory binding should be restricted to only the necessary permissions, limiting the potential impact of credential compromise. Auditing and logging should also be enabled on both the TACACS+ server and the directory service to capture authentication events, failed login attempts, and administrative changes.

Another factor to consider is redundancy and high availability. To ensure continuous authentication services, TACACS+ can be configured with multiple LDAP or Active Directory servers. If the primary directory server becomes unreachable due to maintenance or network issues, the TACACS+ server will automatically attempt to contact the next available server in the list. This failover capability is critical in environments where high availability is mandatory for supporting network operations around the clock.

Integrating TACACS+ with LDAP or Active Directory is also a strategic move for organizations that must comply with regulatory frameworks. By centralizing user authentication through established directory services, organizations can enforce stronger identity governance, reduce administrative complexity, and ensure that AAA processes are aligned with industry best practices. Compliance standards such as PCI DSS, HIPAA, and NIST 800-53 often require centralized identity management, audit trails, and granular access controls, all of which are achievable through this type of integration.

A successful integration project requires close coordination between network security teams, directory service administrators, and IT operations staff. Careful planning and testing are essential to verify that authentication flows function as expected, that group mappings align correctly with TACACS+ authorization policies, and that security configurations meet organizational requirements. By leveraging the strengths of both TACACS+ and LDAP or Active Directory, organizations can create a secure, scalable, and efficient AAA architecture that simplifies identity management while maintaining the robust access control needed to protect critical network assets.

Customizing Authentication Policies

Customizing authentication policies in TACACS+ is a critical task that enables organizations to align their access control mechanisms with their unique operational requirements, security strategies, and compliance obligations. Authentication is not simply about verifying user identity; it is about creating a tailored process that balances security with usability, ensuring that different user roles, devices, and contexts are factored into how authentication is handled across the network. In TACACS+, customization options are highly flexible, giving administrators the power to define detailed authentication workflows that adapt to diverse network environments.

The first step in customizing authentication policies involves defining how users will authenticate when attempting to access network devices or services. TACACS+ supports multiple authentication methods, and administrators must choose the approach that best suits the security posture of the organization. For example, simple password-based authentication may be acceptable in environments with limited exposure, while critical infrastructure may require stronger mechanisms such as two-factor authentication (2FA) or integration with an external identity provider like LDAP or Active Directory. By modifying the TACACS+ configuration file, administrators can specify which authentication method should apply to specific user groups or individual devices, allowing for differentiated policies based on risk level.

One of the key elements in customizing authentication policies is the ability to implement user- or group-specific authentication rules. In TACACS+, user accounts and groups can be defined with distinct authentication requirements, such as varying password complexity rules or additional security measures for privileged users. For example, administrative users who perform high-risk tasks on core network devices may be required to use a stronger authentication method, such as a token-based system, while regular users accessing less sensitive systems might rely on standard credentials. This differentiation ensures that high-value accounts are subject to greater scrutiny without unnecessarily complicating access for lower-risk users.

Customizing authentication policies also involves managing fallback and redundancy options. In some scenarios, the TACACS+ server might be temporarily unreachable due to network issues or maintenance. In such cases, it is common practice to configure fallback authentication mechanisms on client devices, allowing them to revert to local user accounts or an alternate AAA server. Administrators can customize policies to determine under what circumstances fallback methods should be used and which users are allowed to authenticate using these backup options. For instance, local authentication may be permitted only for senior network engineers during outages, while regular users are denied access until full TACACS+ service is restored.

Context-aware authentication is another important aspect of customizing policies. TACACS+ allows administrators to factor in environmental variables such as the location of the user, the device they are connecting from, or the time of day when crafting authentication rules. A common policy might restrict certain user groups to specific working hours, blocking access attempts outside those periods to reduce the risk of unauthorized activities during off-hours. Similarly, administrators may configure policies that permit full access from corporate networks but limit access when connections originate from remote or less-trusted locations. This level of contextual customization helps organizations reduce the attack surface and enforce security controls dynamically based on real-world conditions.

Another layer of customization comes through the integration of TACACS+ with external security solutions such as multi-factor authentication platforms. By combining TACACS+ with an MFA system, administrators can enforce a two-step verification process that requires users to present something they know (a password) and something they have (a one-time token or push notification). This integration provides an added layer of protection, especially for accounts with elevated privileges. Customizing TACACS+ to mandate MFA for all users accessing critical infrastructure strengthens the organization's defenses against credential theft, phishing, and brute force attacks.

Administrators can also tailor authentication policies by defining user privilege levels during the authentication phase. TACACS+ allows administrators to assign privilege levels as part of the authentication response, enabling the client device to immediately apply role-based access controls based on the authenticated user's assigned level. For instance, a policy might specify that users belonging to a certain group are automatically assigned a privilege level of 5, which limits them to monitoring tasks, while users with higher privileges are assigned levels 10 or 15, granting them administrative rights. This seamless link between authentication and access control reduces the risk of human error and streamlines the enforcement of security policies.

Customizing authentication policies is not limited to user identity checks alone; it can also extend to service-based restrictions. TACACS+ allows administrators to define which services a user can access as part of the authentication decision. Services such as login, enable mode, PPP sessions, or administrative shells can be selectively granted or denied based on the user's profile. This service-based control provides another layer of granularity, ensuring that users only gain access to the specific services they require for their duties.

Custom logging and reporting are additional areas where authentication policies can be tailored. TACACS+ enables administrators to define logging levels and specify which authentication events should trigger alerts or detailed logs. For example, authentication attempts from suspicious IP addresses, repeated login failures, or successful authentications outside of normal working hours can be flagged for immediate review. By customizing these logging policies, organizations can enhance their ability to detect and respond to security incidents, ensuring that authentication processes are not only functional but also provide actionable intelligence to security teams.

Periodic reviews and audits are essential to the effectiveness of customized authentication policies. Over time, user roles, infrastructure, and security threats evolve, and authentication policies must be adapted to reflect these changes. Administrators should establish a regular review cycle to assess whether current policies continue to meet organizational needs, address emerging threats, and comply with relevant regulatory standards. This iterative process ensures that TACACS+ authentication policies remain aligned with the organization's security objectives and operational realities.

Customizing authentication policies also contributes significantly to regulatory compliance. Standards such as PCI DSS, HIPAA, and ISO 27001 require organizations to enforce strong access controls, protect sensitive systems, and document user authentication processes. By tailoring TACACS+ authentication policies to meet or exceed these requirements, organizations can demonstrate compliance more easily during audits while simultaneously reinforcing the security of their network infrastructure.

The ability to customize authentication policies within TACACS+ provides organizations with the flexibility and control needed to protect critical assets while maintaining operational efficiency. From role-based and service-based restrictions to multi-factor authentication and context-aware access rules, TACACS+ offers a wide array of customization options. These capabilities empower administrators to build authentication workflows that not only prevent unauthorized access but also support the organization's business goals and security strategy. Careful design, ongoing refinement, and alignment with best practices and compliance mandates ensure that customized authentication policies remain a powerful tool in the organization's broader access control framework.

Role-Based Access Control with TACACS+

Role-Based Access Control, or RBAC, is a critical methodology used by organizations to ensure that users are granted only the level of access necessary to perform their job functions. When applied in conjunction with TACACS+, RBAC becomes an effective way to centralize and enforce security policies across network infrastructure. The RBAC model focuses on assigning permissions to roles rather than individual users, which significantly simplifies the administration of complex networks with multiple devices and users with varying responsibilities. By combining TACACS+ with RBAC, organizations can create a scalable and manageable access control strategy that ensures operational efficiency while minimizing security risks.

In the context of TACACS+, RBAC begins with the definition of user roles within the TACACS+ server configuration. Each role represents a logical grouping of users who share similar access needs and job duties. For example, a typical deployment might include roles such as network administrators, network operators, monitoring staff, and external contractors. Each role is associated with a specific set of permissions that define what tasks members of that role are authorized to perform on network devices. These permissions can include command-level restrictions, privilege levels, and service access controls, allowing for precise and granular policy enforcement.

The process of implementing RBAC with TACACS+ starts with grouping users into roles within the TACACS+ configuration file. This is typically done by defining user groups, each containing a list of users and the associated access rules. Users assigned to a specific group automatically inherit the permissions configured for that group, eliminating the need to define permissions on a per-user basis. For example, all users in the "Network_Operators" group might have read-only access to device configurations, while users in the "Network_Admins" group have full administrative privileges, including the ability to modify configurations and reload devices.

The core of TACACS+ RBAC lies in its command authorization capabilities. TACACS+ allows administrators to create highly specific command authorization policies for each role. These policies determine which commands are allowed, which are denied, and which may require further interaction or approval. This level of control is especially valuable in environments where multiple teams interact with the same network devices but have different responsibilities. For instance, monitoring staff may only need access to diagnostic commands such as show running-config or ping, while administrators require the ability to make configuration changes or apply patches.

TACACS+ RBAC also leverages privilege levels to further enforce role-based permissions. Privilege levels are numeric values that represent different tiers of authority on network devices, often ranging from 0 to 15. By mapping roles to specific privilege levels, administrators can restrict or enable access to certain device functions based on the user's role. A user with a privilege level of 1 may only be able to perform basic read-only functions, while a user with a privilege level of 15 might have unrestricted access to all device commands. TACACS+ returns the assigned privilege level during the authorization process, which is then enforced by the client device, such as a router or switch.

Another advantage of implementing RBAC with TACACS+ is the ability to create device-specific or context-aware policies. In some organizations, different network devices may require different access control rules based on their function or location. TACACS+ enables administrators to define role-based policies that are applied only when users access certain devices. For example, a user in the "DataCenter_Operators" role may have elevated privileges when accessing core data center switches but may have reduced privileges when connecting to branch office routers. This contextual enforcement ensures that users have appropriate permissions depending on the environment in which they are operating.

TACACS+ RBAC also integrates smoothly with external directory services such as LDAP or Active Directory. By aligning TACACS+ groups with groups defined in the directory service, organizations can streamline user management and ensure that access rights are automatically applied based on directory attributes. When a user authenticates via TACACS+, the server can query the directory to determine group membership and then apply the corresponding TACACS+ role and permissions. This integration reduces administrative overhead, simplifies onboarding and offboarding processes, and ensures consistency between identity management systems and network access controls.

Centralized management of RBAC policies within the TACACS+ server offers significant operational benefits. Instead of configuring user accounts and permissions individually on every network device, administrators can define all access policies in one place and have them enforced across the entire network infrastructure. This not only saves time but also reduces the likelihood of misconfigurations and inconsistencies, which could create security vulnerabilities. Updates to roles, such as adding a new command restriction or modifying privilege levels, can be made on the TACACS+ server and instantly apply to all devices using that server for AAA services.

TACACS+ also supports the creation of nested roles or hierarchical structures. In complex organizations, it may be necessary to create multiple tiers within a single role. For example, within the "Network_Admins" role, there could be sub-roles for senior administrators and junior administrators, each with slightly different levels of access. By using conditional logic and advanced configuration techniques, TACACS+ can apply differentiated permissions based on additional factors such as time-of-day restrictions, source IP addresses, or device types, further refining role-based access control mechanisms.

From a security perspective, RBAC in TACACS+ is essential for reducing the risk of privilege escalation and unauthorized access. By assigning only the minimum necessary permissions to each role, organizations reduce the potential impact of compromised credentials or insider threats. If a user account is compromised, an attacker will only be able to operate within the limited scope of that user's assigned role. This granular control, combined with robust auditing and accounting features, ensures that suspicious activity can be detected quickly and that all user actions are traceable to a specific role and individual.

RBAC is also vital in supporting compliance with industry regulations and standards. Frameworks such as PCI DSS, ISO 27001, and NIST 800-53 emphasize the importance of enforcing least privilege and maintaining clear separation of duties. By leveraging TACACS+ to implement RBAC, organizations can demonstrate adherence to these requirements and provide auditors with detailed evidence of how access controls are applied and maintained across network infrastructure.

The deployment of RBAC using TACACS+ allows for scalable, flexible, and secure access control in environments of all sizes. Whether applied to a small enterprise or a global network spanning thousands of devices, TACACS+ RBAC helps organizations maintain control over who can access network devices and what actions they are permitted to perform. This control is critical for safeguarding network stability, preventing accidental or unauthorized changes, and ensuring that operational and security policies are consistently enforced. The result is a network environment that is not only secure but also easier to manage, even as the organization grows and evolves.

Implementing Command Authorization

Implementing command authorization is a crucial step in enhancing network security and operational control within TACACS+ environments. Command authorization allows organizations to dictate precisely which commands a user or group of users can execute on network devices after successfully authenticating. This granular control is vital in preventing unauthorized actions, accidental misconfigurations, and malicious activities that could compromise the stability or security of network infrastructure. By restricting access to specific commands based on job roles or user profiles, organizations enforce the principle of least privilege while enabling operational efficiency.

The process of implementing command authorization in TACACS+ begins at the configuration level, where administrators define detailed authorization policies in the TACACS+ server's configuration file. These policies specify which commands are allowed or denied for specific users or groups. When a user attempts to execute a command on a network device, the device sends an authorization request to the TACACS+ server, including the user's identity, the privilege level, and the exact command being requested. The TACACS+ server processes this request and responds with an authorization decision based on the configured policy.

TACACS+ command authorization can be applied at various levels of granularity. Administrators can choose to permit or deny entire command sets, specific command keywords, or even particular command parameters. For example, a network technician might be allowed to run show commands for diagnostic purposes but be denied access to configuration mode or any commands that could modify device settings. This level of specificity ensures that users only have the exact capabilities required for their role, reducing the risk of human error or internal threats.

One of the advantages of TACACS+ is its ability to handle command authorization independently of authentication and accounting processes. This separation enables administrators to craft finely tuned policies without altering how users are authenticated or how their activities are logged. For instance, even if two users authenticate successfully using the same credentials or method, their command-level permissions can differ significantly based on the group or role assigned to them in the TACACS+ server configuration.

Command authorization in TACACS+ relies heavily on regular expressions or exact command matching. Administrators define policies by creating rules that match command strings issued by users on network devices. The rules may include wildcards, allowing for broader or more restricted permissions depending on operational needs. For example, an administrator could permit all show commands using a wildcard pattern such as show.*, while denying access to configuration commands like configure terminal or interface commands that might impact the functioning of critical systems.

It is common to structure command authorization policies around user groups to streamline management. By assigning users to groups such as admins, operators, or auditors, organizations can apply consistent command restrictions to multiple users simultaneously. Each group can have a unique set of permitted and denied commands tailored to the duties and responsibilities of its members. For example, operators may have access to operational commands like show interfaces or clear counters, while admins may be allowed full configuration and troubleshooting commands, including the ability to reload devices or apply updates.

The implementation of command authorization also provides the flexibility to enforce contextual controls. Policies can vary based on the network device being accessed, the time of day, or even the IP address of the user's workstation. For example, an organization may permit certain commands during scheduled maintenance windows but restrict them during regular business hours. Alternatively, users connecting from a trusted internal IP range might receive broader permissions than those connecting from remote locations over a VPN. By leveraging these contextual variables, TACACS+ command authorization policies can adapt to operational workflows and security requirements dynamically.

Command authorization is also tightly integrated with the privilege level system in most network devices. When a user attempts to execute a command, the device not only checks with the TACACS+ server but also considers the user's assigned privilege level. The TACACS+ server can enforce policies that assign users to specific privilege levels based on their roles, which the device then uses to control access to certain modes or command sets. Combining privilege levels with command authorization enhances security by creating a dual-layer control model where commands are restricted both by privilege level and by explicit TACACS+ policies.

Detailed logging and accounting are essential components of command authorization implementation. Every authorization request, including allowed and denied commands, should be logged and reviewed regularly. These logs provide valuable audit trails that can reveal policy violations, attempted privilege escalations, or other suspicious activities. By examining authorization logs, security teams can identify trends such as users frequently attempting to execute restricted commands, which may indicate training gaps or potential insider threats.

When implementing command authorization, thorough testing is critical. Administrators should validate that policies function as expected, ensuring that users have access to all required commands without inadvertently restricting essential operations. Testing should include different user roles, devices, and scenarios, including failure conditions such as TACACS+ server outages where fallback mechanisms might be triggered. Many organizations conduct pilot deployments on a subset of devices before rolling out policies network-wide to minimize disruptions and fine-tune policies based on feedback from technical teams.

Training is another key element in the successful implementation of command authorization. Users must be aware of the commands they are permitted to use and the rationale behind these restrictions. Clear documentation of policies and procedures helps prevent confusion and reduces the likelihood of users attempting unauthorized actions. Administrators should also establish escalation procedures for situations where additional permissions are needed temporarily, such as during emergency maintenance or incident response efforts.

Integrating TACACS+ command authorization with other security tools further strengthens the organization's access control framework. For example, combining TACACS+ with a Security Information and Event Management (SIEM) system allows for real-time analysis and alerting based on command authorization events. If a user attempts to execute a restricted command or if multiple failed authorization requests occur within a short timeframe, automated alerts can notify security teams for immediate investigation.

Command authorization with TACACS+ is a fundamental control that enhances accountability and precision in network device management. By enforcing strict, role-based command restrictions, organizations reduce their exposure to operational errors, insider threats, and unauthorized changes. The flexibility and granularity provided by TACACS+ enable administrators to craft customized policies that align with business objectives while supporting compliance with industry standards and regulatory requirements. With careful planning, rigorous testing, and ongoing monitoring, command authorization becomes a powerful tool in maintaining the integrity, availability, and security of critical network infrastructure.

Advanced Accounting for Network Devices

Advanced accounting for network devices using TACACS+ provides organizations with detailed visibility into administrative activities, enabling precise monitoring, compliance, and forensic investigation capabilities. While basic accounting logs standard session events, advanced accounting expands this by capturing highly granular data about every user action, creating a comprehensive audit trail of who accessed what, when, and how. In an era where regulatory compliance and security are critical concerns, advanced accounting serves as a vital tool for maintaining accountability and safeguarding the integrity of the network infrastructure.

TACACS+ accounting operates as one of the three core components of the AAA framework, alongside authentication and authorization. While authentication confirms a user's identity and authorization governs their permissions, accounting records all relevant data about user sessions and actions. Advanced accounting enhances this process by ensuring that not only the start and stop of sessions are logged but also each command entered, each privilege escalation attempted, and each configuration modification applied during the session.

The accounting process begins when a user logs into a network device, such as a router, switch, firewall, or access point. At this stage, the TACACS+ client on the device generates an accounting start record, capturing initial session data including the username, login timestamp, IP address of the user, and the service type (for example, console, SSH, or Telnet). Throughout the user session, the TACACS+ client continues to send accounting data to the TACACS+ server, detailing every significant event. This includes interim updates, such as session status and resource consumption, and command accounting, which logs every command executed by the user, along with its success or failure status.

Advanced accounting with TACACS+ also supports capturing information about privilege level changes. When a user attempts to escalate their privilege level within the device, such as entering privileged EXEC mode or global configuration mode, the TACACS+ client records this event and sends it to the accounting server. This is crucial for detecting unauthorized or unexpected privilege escalations, which may signal insider threats, policy violations, or compromised accounts.

Command accounting is one of the most powerful features of advanced TACACS+ accounting. Each command a user executes is logged individually, including the exact syntax used and the context in which it was run. This level of detail allows organizations to reconstruct the entire session history, identifying actions such as viewing configurations, modifying routing tables, reloading devices, or applying firewall rule changes. Command accounting helps enforce operational discipline by making it clear that every action is traceable, thereby encouraging adherence to security policies and discouraging careless or malicious behavior.

In highly regulated industries such as finance, healthcare, and critical infrastructure, advanced accounting helps organizations meet stringent audit and compliance requirements. Frameworks such as PCI DSS, HIPAA, NERC CIP, and ISO 27001 require detailed logging of all administrative activity on systems that handle sensitive data or critical operations. TACACS+ accounting records can be exported to centralized log management solutions or SIEM platforms to ensure secure long-term storage and to enable correlation with other security events across the environment. The ability to provide auditors with complete records of user sessions, down to the individual commands executed, demonstrates strong governance and supports audit readiness.

Advanced accounting also aids in incident response and forensic investigations. When a security incident occurs, such as a network outage or a suspected breach, reviewing TACACS+ accounting logs can reveal which user accounts accessed specific devices, what commands were executed, and when the actions occurred. This forensic capability enables security teams to rapidly identify the root cause of incidents, trace the sequence of events leading up to them, and take corrective measures to prevent recurrence. Moreover, when combined with real-time monitoring systems, advanced accounting data can generate automated alerts for suspicious activities, such as the execution of dangerous commands outside of approved maintenance windows.

Another key aspect of advanced accounting is session duration tracking and resource usage monitoring. TACACS+ accounting records the exact time when users log in and log out, providing a clear picture of session lengths and user productivity. In environments where remote access is frequent, such as organizations with distributed workforces or third-party contractors, session duration tracking ensures that users are not connected for longer than necessary, reducing the risk of unattended sessions or resource misuse.

Advanced accounting in TACACS+ also supports policy enforcement through session attribute tracking. Organizations can configure accounting policies to collect specific session attributes such as the client IP address, access method, device hostname, and access protocol. This information can be analyzed to identify patterns such as users consistently logging in from unusual IP ranges, using outdated protocols, or connecting to unauthorized devices. By combining session attributes with command-level logs, organizations gain a holistic view of network usage and user behavior.

For large organizations or service providers managing multiple client networks, advanced TACACS+ accounting provides the necessary tools to implement multi-tenancy and customer-specific auditing. By segmenting accounting data based on device groups, user groups, or organizational units, service providers can generate individualized audit reports for each customer or internal business unit. This ensures that accounting data remains organized, relevant, and tailored to specific compliance and operational requirements.

Automation and reporting are also integral to advanced accounting practices. By integrating TACACS+ accounting logs with automation tools, organizations can generate regular reports detailing user activities, policy compliance metrics, and security anomalies. These reports provide valuable insights to management and technical teams, supporting proactive risk management and continuous improvement initiatives. For example, weekly or monthly reports may highlight trends such as repeated command denial events, unusually long session durations, or excessive privilege escalations, prompting further investigation and corrective action.

Performance optimization is an important consideration when implementing advanced accounting on network devices. High volumes of accounting data can introduce overhead on both the TACACS+ server and the client devices. To mitigate this, administrators should ensure that the TACACS+ server infrastructure is properly scaled, with sufficient CPU, memory, and storage to handle peak loads. Additionally, accounting policies can be fine-tuned to balance detail with performance, ensuring that critical commands and events are always logged without overwhelming the system with excessive data.

Advanced accounting with TACACS+ is a critical element in modern network security and compliance frameworks. By capturing and analyzing comprehensive user activity data, organizations gain actionable intelligence that supports secure operations, regulatory compliance, and effective incident response. The ability to log every session event, privilege change, and executed command creates a powerful layer of accountability, helping to protect both the network and the organization's broader digital assets. With careful configuration, integration, and monitoring, advanced accounting elevates TACACS+ from a basic access control mechanism to a cornerstone of enterprise security governance.

TACACS+ Logging and Event Analysis

TACACS+ logging and event analysis play a crucial role in network security by providing a transparent and detailed record of all administrative actions taken on network devices. These logs not only enable administrators to track user activities but also serve as valuable assets for auditing, troubleshooting, and enhancing security operations. The ability to capture, analyze, and interpret TACACS+ logs is an essential aspect of maintaining robust network access control, ensuring compliance with regulatory frameworks, and quickly identifying any unusual or unauthorized activity that could pose a threat to the infrastructure.

At the heart of TACACS+ logging is the principle of capturing detailed records for every event related to authentication, authorization, and accounting. TACACS+ clients, which include network devices like routers, switches, firewalls, and wireless access points, send these events to a centralized TACACS+ server. The server logs every request, including login attempts, successful authentications, failed logins, privilege level changes, command executions, and session start/stop times. By capturing this data, TACACS+ ensures that all administrative actions are logged for future review, which is particularly critical in environments that require strict security and compliance controls.

TACACS+ logs typically include a wide range of information for each event. For authentication events, the logs record the user's identity, the IP address of the device from which the user attempted to connect, the service type used (such as SSH, Telnet, or console), and the result of the authentication attempt (success or failure). For authorization events, logs include the specific commands that were requested, whether they were permitted or denied, and the reason for any denial. Similarly, accounting logs capture session details such as session duration, resource usage, and the commands executed by the user during the session. This level of detail ensures that every action taken by a user is fully traceable, which is vital for operational auditing and forensic investigations.

One of the most important benefits of TACACS+ logging is its role in real-time event analysis. By continuously collecting data from all network devices, administrators can monitor the network for suspicious behavior or policy violations as they happen. For example, if a user attempts to access a restricted command or escalates their privileges unexpectedly, these actions will be logged and flagged in real-time. Security information and event management (SIEM) systems often integrate with TACACS+ logging to automate the detection of anomalies and generate alerts. These alerts can help administrators quickly respond to potential security incidents, such as unauthorized access attempts, misconfigurations, or other breaches.

In addition to real-time analysis, logging and event analysis provide significant historical value. In the event of a security incident or system failure, administrators can analyze past logs to determine the root cause of the issue. For example, if a network breach is detected, the logs can reveal which user account was involved, what actions were taken, which devices were accessed, and whether there were any signs of privilege escalation. This forensic capability is crucial for investigating the incident and mitigating future risks. Furthermore, it allows organizations to provide a detailed report for internal investigations, compliance audits, or legal inquiries.

The data captured by TACACS+ logging is also essential for meeting regulatory and industry compliance standards. Many regulations, including PCI DSS, HIPAA, and GDPR, require organizations to maintain detailed records of administrative access and to implement strong auditing mechanisms. TACACS+ logging helps fulfill these requirements by ensuring that all actions taken on critical devices are logged and easily accessible. These logs also help organizations demonstrate adherence to security best practices and provide evidence of due diligence in the event of a compliance audit or breach investigation.

Effective event analysis depends not only on logging the data but also on properly analyzing and interpreting it. Raw log files can quickly become overwhelming, especially in large organizations with complex network infrastructures. For this reason, many organizations turn to centralized logging systems or SIEM solutions to aggregate and analyze TACACS+ logs. These systems can automatically correlate log entries from multiple devices, search for patterns, and identify trends that would be difficult to spot manually. For example, a SIEM system might detect multiple failed login attempts from the same IP address, flagging this as a potential brute force attack. Similarly, the system can alert administrators if a user suddenly gains access to high-privilege commands or if commands are executed outside normal working hours.

TACACS+ logs can be further enriched by adding metadata to the entries, such as device identifiers, geographic locations, or business unit information. By associating these additional data points with log events, administrators can gain even more context and insight into the actions being taken across the network. For instance, if a user logs in from a location outside of their usual geographic region, the log entry could be marked with the user's usual location, raising a red flag for further investigation.

For organizations that require high levels of data retention, TACACS+ logs can be configured to store records for long periods of time, ensuring that historical data is available for auditing or legal purposes. However, retaining large volumes of log data can present challenges in terms of storage and retrieval. To address this, many organizations implement data lifecycle management policies that archive older logs in a more cost-effective storage medium, while keeping recent logs readily accessible for real-time analysis. Additionally, log data should be securely encrypted to prevent unauthorized access, particularly for sensitive environments such as healthcare, finance, or government sectors.

While logging and event analysis provide numerous benefits, it is important to configure and manage TACACS+ logging correctly to ensure the logs are both accurate and useful. Administrators must ensure that the logging level is appropriately set to capture the necessary events without overwhelming the system with excessive data. In some cases, administrators may choose to log only critical events, such as failed logins or command denials, while in other environments, it may be necessary to log every command executed for complete auditing. Balancing the need for detailed information with system performance is a key consideration in any logging configuration.

Moreover, TACACS+ logs should be periodically reviewed to ensure they are providing the necessary insights and are not being overwritten or lost due to storage limitations. Regular audits of logging practices and stored data help ensure that logs are complete, accurate, and compliant with organizational and regulatory requirements. By establishing clear log management policies, organizations can maintain effective logging systems that provide reliable data for event analysis, security monitoring, and compliance reporting.

TACACS+ logging and event analysis are fundamental to ensuring the security, integrity, and compliance of network infrastructures. By capturing and analyzing detailed records of all user activities, organizations can maintain a transparent view of network operations, identify potential threats in real-time, and meet stringent regulatory requirements. The ability to monitor and audit administrative actions across all network devices strengthens the overall security posture, helping organizations quickly identify and respond to unauthorized or suspicious activity, while also providing essential documentation for compliance purposes.

Troubleshooting TACACS+ Deployments

Troubleshooting TACACS+ deployments is a critical skill for network administrators, as it ensures that the authentication, authorization, and accounting processes function smoothly across network devices. While TACACS+ is a reliable protocol, issues can arise due to misconfigurations, network disruptions, or software bugs. Understanding the common problems that can occur and having the knowledge to resolve them is essential for maintaining security, uptime, and operational efficiency in an organization's network infrastructure.

The first step in troubleshooting a TACACS+ deployment is to verify that the basic network connectivity between the TACACS+ client (such as a router or switch) and the TACACS+ server is functional. A common issue can be network-related, where the client cannot reach the server due to incorrect IP addresses, misconfigured firewall rules, or routing problems. Administrators should ensure that both the TACACS+ server and client are on the same network or that proper routing exists between the devices. A simple tool like the ping command can quickly confirm whether the client can reach the server over the network. If pinging the server fails, network connectivity should be checked thoroughly by investigating any routing issues, ACLs, or firewall configurations that may be blocking the communication.

Once basic connectivity is confirmed, the next step is to verify that the TACACS+ server is running and able to accept requests. If the TACACS+ server is down or unresponsive, authentication requests from network devices will fail. Administrators should check the status of the TACACS+ service on the server, ensuring that the TACACS+ daemon (such as tac_plus on Linux-based systems) is active and running. In many cases, the service might have failed to start due to misconfigurations, resource limitations, or software errors. System logs on the server should be examined for any errors related to the

TACACS+ service or related dependencies. Additionally, checking whether the correct ports (usually TCP port 49) are open and not blocked by any firewall is important.

If the TACACS+ server is running and reachable but authentication requests still fail, the next logical step is to review the server's configuration. One common issue is a mismatch in the shared secret used between the TACACS+ server and its clients. The shared secret is critical for encrypting and decrypting communication between the client and the server, and if there is a discrepancy in the configured secret on either side, authentication requests will not be successfully processed. Administrators should carefully verify that the shared secret is correctly configured on both the TACACS+ client and server. Any differences in this secret will lead to failed authentication attempts.

A misconfiguration of user credentials or authentication settings is another frequent cause of TACACS+ issues. If a user is unable to authenticate, administrators should verify the credentials stored on the server or integrated directory services such as LDAP or Active Directory. Common problems can include incorrect usernames, expired passwords, or misconfigured attributes. The configuration files of the TACACS+ server should be checked for any errors in the definitions of user accounts, groups, or access policies. Additionally, if the TACACS+ server is integrated with an external directory service, it is important to ensure that the connection to the directory is active and properly configured. Any issues with the external directory service, such as server outages or incorrect binding credentials, will prevent successful authentication through TACACS+.

Authorization failures are another area where troubleshooting is essential. If a user is authenticated but is denied access to specific commands or resources, the issue often lies in the authorization policies defined on the TACACS+ server. TACACS+ allows for highly granular command-level authorization, and misconfigurations in these policies can prevent users from executing necessary commands. Administrators should verify that the authorization rules defined for each user or user group are correct. This includes checking that the privilege levels assigned to users match the intended access rights and that command authorization is properly configured to allow the necessary commands. A common issue could be overly restrictive policies that inadvertently block valid actions.

Accounting issues can also arise in TACACS+ deployments, particularly if accounting records are not being generated or transmitted correctly. If the client device is not sending accounting information to the TACACS+ server, administrators should first check that accounting has been enabled on both the client and the server. On the client side, the TACACS+ configuration file should have the correct accounting settings, ensuring that session start, stop, and interim updates are properly configured. On the server side, the accounting server logs should be reviewed to verify that the data is being recorded. If the server is not receiving accounting data, network issues, such as dropped packets or firewall restrictions, could be the cause. Additionally, the server's storage capacity should be checked to ensure that logs are not being discarded due to insufficient space.

For more advanced troubleshooting, administrators can enable debug logging on the TACACS+ server to gain deeper insights into the problem. Debug logs provide detailed information about the interaction between the client and the server, including the flow of authentication, authorization, and accounting requests. By enabling debug mode, administrators can see exactly where the process is failing—whether it is during the authentication phase, when the authorization decision is being made, or during the accounting phase. Debugging can also provide information about errors or miscommunications that are not readily apparent in standard logs, helping to identify issues such as packet corruption, timeouts, or protocol mismatches.

If troubleshooting continues to be difficult, administrators can turn to network capture tools such as Wireshark to analyze the traffic between the TACACS+ client and server. This allows for the inspection of the actual TACACS+ packets being sent and received, which can provide insights into communication issues, incorrect packet formats, or network-related problems. Network captures are especially useful in diagnosing issues related to encryption, as administrators can verify that packets are properly encrypted and contain the correct data.

Lastly, it is important to consider that TACACS+ deployments are often part of a broader security infrastructure that includes other protocols such as RADIUS, LDAP, or VPN services. In environments with complex setups, problems may not always originate from the TACACS+ configuration itself but from how it interacts with other systems. Integration issues, such as misconfigured RADIUS fallbacks, LDAP server connectivity issues, or VPN-related authentication failures, can complicate troubleshooting efforts. Administrators should ensure that all components of the network security infrastructure are properly configured and that they communicate with each other as expected.

Through careful diagnosis and methodical troubleshooting, most issues within TACACS+ deployments can be identified and resolved. It requires a combination of network knowledge, server configuration expertise, and familiarity with the TACACS+ protocol to efficiently detect and fix problems that may arise. By addressing network connectivity, server settings, credential configurations, and policy definitions, administrators can ensure that TACACS+ provides a secure, reliable, and efficient method for controlling access to network resources.

Secure TACACS+ Communication over Networks

Securing TACACS+ communication over networks is a fundamental aspect of ensuring the integrity, confidentiality, and availability of network access control systems. TACACS+ is a widely adopted protocol for centralized authentication, authorization, and accounting (AAA) services that manage administrative access to critical network devices such as routers, switches, firewalls, and wireless access points. Since TACACS+ is responsible for processing sensitive administrative data, it is essential to secure the communication channels between clients and servers to protect against interception, tampering, and unauthorized access.

The most prominent feature of TACACS+ communication security is its use of encryption. Unlike its counterpart RADIUS, which encrypts only the user password, TACACS+ encrypts the entire payload of its packets. This includes not only authentication credentials but also authorization data, command strings, and accounting information. The encryption of the full packet ensures that all sensitive information, including usernames, passwords, and executed commands, is protected from eavesdropping and unauthorized access during transmission. By encrypting the entire communication, TACACS+ provides an added layer of security in environments where protecting sensitive data is paramount.

TACACS+ uses TCP (Transmission Control Protocol) as its transport protocol, which adds another layer of security compared to RADIUS, which uses UDP (User Datagram Protocol). TCP's connection-oriented nature ensures reliable, ordered delivery of packets, which is crucial for maintaining the integrity of the authentication process. TCP also allows for error detection and retransmission in case of packet loss, providing a more robust mechanism for communication. This reliability is particularly important in environments where authentication, authorization, and accounting data must be accurately transmitted to ensure proper network access control. The use of TCP in TACACS+ also mitigates certain risks associated with UDP, such as the possibility of packets being dropped or lost without detection.

Another important aspect of securing TACACS+ communication is the use of a shared secret. The shared secret is a key that is pre-configured on both the TACACS+ server and its client devices. This secret is used to encrypt and decrypt the data exchanged between the two entities. The strength of the shared secret is critical to the security of the communication. A weak or easily guessable secret could expose the communication to brute force attacks, potentially compromising the entire access control system. Therefore, it is essential to use a strong, complex shared secret that is kept confidential. Additionally, the shared secret should be changed periodically to minimize the risk of exposure.

To further enhance the security of TACACS+ communication, administrators should implement transport layer security (TLS) or IPsec tunneling to encrypt the entire session, not just the TACACS+ protocol itself. These additional encryption layers can help secure the data as it travels over the network, especially when the network traverses untrusted segments or the internet. IPsec, for example, provides a robust method for encrypting all traffic between devices, including TACACS+ packets. This layered security model ensures that even if an attacker gains access to the network infrastructure, they would be unable to decipher or manipulate the data being exchanged between the TACACS+ clients and servers.

The physical security of the network infrastructure also plays a role in securing TACACS+ communication. In enterprise networks, the physical environment where the TACACS+ server and client devices are located should be protected from unauthorized access. Physical security measures such as access control systems, surveillance, and secure server rooms can prevent attackers from gaining direct access to network devices and potentially compromising the shared secrets or configuration files that could undermine the security of TACACS+ communications.

Moreover, network segmentation and firewall configurations are crucial in securing TACACS+ communication. TACACS+ servers should be isolated in secure subnets, and firewalls should be configured to restrict access to the server only from trusted IP addresses. For instance, only network devices that need to authenticate or perform administrative functions should be allowed to send requests to the TACACS+ server. This minimizes the attack surface and prevents unauthorized devices from trying to communicate with the server. Additionally, firewall rules should be set up to allow only the required ports (typically TCP port 49) and block all other unnecessary traffic to and from the TACACS+ server.

Access control lists (ACLs) can also be implemented on the TACACS+ server to restrict which devices or IP addresses are allowed to communicate with it. These ACLs provide an additional layer of protection by ensuring that only authorized network devices are capable of initiating TACACS+ authentication requests. This prevents unauthorized devices from attempting to authenticate or access sensitive data stored on the TACACS+ server. By using a combination of ACLs and firewall rules, administrators can further tighten the security of TACACS+ communication, limiting the risk of external attacks.

Monitoring and logging are essential for maintaining the security of TACACS+ communication. By configuring detailed logging on both the TACACS+ server and client devices, administrators can track every authentication attempt, authorization decision, and accounting record generated during user sessions. These logs should be regularly reviewed for signs of suspicious activity, such as failed authentication attempts, privilege escalation attempts, or unauthorized access from unfamiliar IP addresses. Integration with a Security Information and Event Management (SIEM) system can further enhance security by automatically correlating events across the network and alerting administrators to potential threats in real-time.

Regular security audits are also an essential part of maintaining secure TACACS+ communication. Administrators should periodically review the TACACS+ configuration, shared secret management practices, and network security posture to ensure that they are following best practices. Audits can help identify vulnerabilities, such as weak passwords, outdated encryption algorithms, or misconfigured access controls, that could expose TACACS+ communication to attacks. By conducting regular audits and updates, organizations can stay ahead of evolving security threats and maintain a strong security posture.

In high-risk environments, additional security measures such as multi-factor authentication (MFA) can be implemented alongside TACACS+ to further secure the authentication process. By requiring users to provide multiple forms of verification—such as a password and a one-time token or biometrics—organizations can add an extra layer of protection against unauthorized access. MFA can be seamlessly integrated into TACACS+ workflows, ensuring that only users who pass multiple verification checks are allowed to access network resources.

Securing TACACS+ communication is a vital aspect of any organization's network security strategy. By implementing encryption, using strong shared secrets, deploying TLS or IPsec for additional protection, configuring access controls, and employing monitoring tools, organizations can safeguard the integrity of their authentication, authorization, and accounting processes. Secure TACACS+ communication ensures that only authorized users are granted access to critical network devices and that all administrative actions are recorded and protected from tampering or interception. With the right security measures in place, organizations can confidently rely on TACACS+ to manage access control across their network infrastructure.

High Availability and Redundancy

High availability and redundancy are essential concepts in ensuring the continuous operation of critical network infrastructure, especially when dealing with access control systems like TACACS+. Given the central role that TACACS+ plays in managing authentication, authorization, and accounting (AAA) for network devices, ensuring that the TACACS+ service is always available is crucial for maintaining security and operational efficiency across the network. A disruption in TACACS+ services can prevent network administrators from accessing devices for troubleshooting, configuration, or monitoring, which can lead to downtime, security risks, and operational inefficiencies. By implementing high availability and redundancy, organizations can minimize the risk of service interruptions, improve the reliability of their network access control, and ensure that TACACS+ continues to function even in the event of hardware failures, network outages, or other unforeseen circumstances.

To achieve high availability and redundancy for TACACS+ services, it is necessary to implement multiple strategies, including server failover, load balancing, and disaster recovery plans. One of the most common and effective methods is the use of multiple TACACS+ servers configured in an active-passive or active-active deployment model. In an active-passive configuration, one server handles all authentication, authorization, and accounting requests, while the other server remains on standby, ready to take over in the event of a failure. This setup ensures that there is always a backup server available to handle requests if the primary server goes down. The failover process is typically seamless, with the backup server automatically assuming the role of the primary server without requiring manual intervention.

In contrast, an active-active configuration involves multiple TACACS+ servers running concurrently, sharing the load of authentication, authorization, and accounting requests. This model distributes the workload across multiple servers, reducing the burden on any single server and ensuring that if one server becomes overloaded or fails, the remaining servers can continue processing requests. This setup improves both performance and reliability by providing a distributed system that can handle a higher volume of requests and maintain service availability even if one or more servers experience issues.

Regardless of whether an active-passive or active-active configuration is chosen, it is important to implement load balancing between the TACACS+ servers to ensure that the distribution of requests is handled efficiently. Load balancing can be achieved through hardware or software solutions, and it works by directing incoming authentication requests to the least-loaded or most available server. This ensures that each TACACS+ server is used optimally, preventing overloading of any single server and maintaining a smooth, uninterrupted service. In the event that one server becomes unavailable, the load balancer can automatically reroute traffic to the remaining servers, ensuring that users and network devices are still able to authenticate and access the network without disruption.

Redundancy also extends beyond the TACACS+ servers themselves to include the network infrastructure that supports them. The network paths between TACACS+ clients (such as routers, switches, and firewalls) and the TACACS+ servers should be configured for redundancy to prevent single points of failure. This can be accomplished by using multiple network links, spanning tree protocols to prevent network loops, and implementing dynamic routing protocols that automatically reroute traffic if one path becomes unavailable. By ensuring that there are multiple physical and logical paths for TACACS+ traffic to travel, organizations can prevent network outages from affecting the availability of the TACACS+ service.

In addition to ensuring redundancy in the network and servers, organizations must also consider redundancy in the backend systems used for TACACS+ authentication, such as directory services like LDAP or Active Directory. If these systems go down, TACACS+ authentication requests cannot be processed, even if the TACACS+ servers themselves are functioning properly. Therefore, it is critical to deploy multiple, redundant instances of LDAP or Active Directory servers, as well as ensure that these systems are synchronized and regularly updated to avoid conflicts or data inconsistencies. The redundancy of backend systems can be achieved using database replication, clustering, or other high-availability technologies, ensuring that TACACS+ continues to function even in the event of an LDAP or Active Directory failure.

Regular monitoring and testing are essential components of any high availability and redundancy strategy. Organizations should continuously monitor the health of their TACACS+ servers, load balancers, network paths, and backend systems. This can be achieved using monitoring tools that track system performance, server availability, and network latency. Alerts should be configured to notify administrators of any issues that might impact the availability of TACACS+ services, such as server failures, network interruptions, or excessive load. Periodic failover testing should also be conducted to ensure that the failover mechanisms are functioning as expected and that the system can handle server failures or network disruptions without affecting the user experience.

Disaster recovery planning is also a critical aspect of high availability and redundancy. While failover and load balancing help mitigate the impact of server or network issues, organizations must also prepare for worst-case scenarios, such as the complete failure of a data center or the loss of a region. A well-designed disaster recovery plan ensures that TACACS+ services can be quickly restored in the event of a major outage. This may involve setting up geographically distributed servers or using cloud-based services for additional redundancy. Data backups should be regularly performed to ensure that all TACACS+ configuration and accounting data can be restored in case of data loss. Moreover, organizations should have clear procedures in place for restoring services, including which team members are responsible for initiating failover or recovery actions and how communication will be handled during an outage.

Security considerations are also an important part of implementing high availability and redundancy for TACACS+ deployments. Redundant servers and network links should be properly secured to prevent unauthorized access or attacks. Encryption protocols should be used to protect the integrity and confidentiality of TACACS+ traffic, especially if the servers are deployed across different geographic locations or over the internet. Firewalls, access control lists (ACLs), and VPNs should be used to restrict access to the TACACS+ servers and ensure that only authorized devices can communicate with them. Redundant systems should be regularly tested for vulnerabilities and patched to ensure that they remain secure.

High availability and redundancy are critical for ensuring the reliability and resilience of TACACS+ deployments in enterprise networks. By implementing strategies such as multiple TACACS+ servers, load balancing, redundant network paths, and backend system redundancy, organizations can ensure that their access control systems remain operational, even in the face of hardware failures, network issues, or other disruptions. Regular monitoring, testing, and disaster recovery planning are essential to maintaining the integrity of these systems and minimizing the impact of any potential outages. With a robust high availability and redundancy strategy in place, organizations can maintain secure and uninterrupted access to network resources while minimizing the risks associated with service disruptions.

Load Balancing TACACS+ Servers

Load balancing is a crucial component of ensuring the scalability, reliability, and availability of TACACS+ deployments in large enterprise or service provider environments. TACACS+ is widely used for centralized authentication, authorization, and accounting (AAA) across network devices, and as such, its servers must be able to handle large volumes of requests from multiple clients. When TACACS+ servers are not load-balanced, a single server may become overwhelmed by excessive requests, leading to delays, service interruptions, or even system failures. By implementing load balancing for TACACS+ servers, organizations can distribute the authentication load more evenly, improve system performance, and increase redundancy, all of which contribute to a more robust and resilient network access control system.

The concept of load balancing involves distributing incoming traffic across multiple servers to ensure that no single server becomes a bottleneck. In the context of TACACS+, this means that user authentication requests, authorization requests, and accounting data are distributed across multiple TACACS+ servers. Each server performs the same function, and the load balancer decides which server should handle each request based on various factors such as server load, performance, and availability. By spreading the load across multiple servers, organizations can ensure that their TACACS+ infrastructure remains responsive and capable of handling high volumes of traffic without degradation in service.

There are several methods for implementing load balancing with TACACS+ servers, depending on the organization's needs and infrastructure. One of the most common approaches is to use a hardware load balancer, which is placed between the TACACS+ clients (such as network devices) and the TACACS+ servers. The load balancer is responsible for receiving incoming authentication requests from network devices and forwarding them to one of the available TACACS+ servers. The load balancer can use various algorithms, such as round-robin, least connections, or weighted least connections, to determine which server should handle each request. Round-robin is a simple algorithm that distributes requests evenly across all available servers, while least connections sends requests to the server with the fewest active connections, ensuring that no server is overloaded.

In addition to hardware load balancers, software-based load balancing solutions can also be used. These solutions often run on general-purpose servers and can be integrated with existing network infrastructure. Software load balancing provides flexibility and cost-effectiveness, especially in environments where hardware load balancers may be too expensive or unnecessary. Software-based solutions typically offer similar features to hardware load balancers, such as the ability to choose between various load balancing algorithms and to monitor server health in real-time. One advantage of software load balancers is that they can be easily scaled to handle growing traffic volumes, making them suitable for dynamic and evolving network environments.

For TACACS+ servers, load balancing can also be achieved at the DNS (Domain Name System) level. In this approach, the DNS server can be configured to return different IP addresses for the TACACS+ server domain, thereby distributing requests across multiple servers. This is known as DNS round-robin load balancing. While this method is relatively simple to set up, it has its limitations. For example, DNS-based load balancing does not provide advanced features such as session persistence or automatic failover in case of server failure. As a result, while DNS load balancing can be a useful tool for distributing traffic in smaller deployments, it is often used in conjunction with more advanced hardware or software load balancers for larger, more complex environments.

One of the key considerations when implementing load balancing for TACACS+ servers is session persistence. Session persistence, also known as "sticky sessions," ensures that once a user's request is routed to a particular server, all subsequent requests from that user are handled by the same server throughout the duration of their session. This is important because TACACS+ relies on maintaining session state, including user authentication data, privilege levels, and command authorization information. If a user is routed to different servers during a single session, the session state may be lost, causing authentication failures or inconsistent authorization responses. To achieve session persistence, load balancers must be configured to track sessions and ensure that requests from the same user or device are always forwarded to the same TACACS+ server.

Another critical factor to consider when setting up load balancing for TACACS+ is server health monitoring. A load balancer should continuously monitor the health of the TACACS+ servers to ensure that traffic is only directed to servers that are functioning properly. If a server becomes unresponsive or encounters an error, the load balancer should automatically reroute traffic to healthy servers, ensuring minimal disruption to service. Health checks can be performed using various methods, such as checking server response times, monitoring CPU and memory usage, or sending test authentication requests to the server. These health checks should be frequent and automated to quickly detect and respond to server failures.

In addition to ensuring the availability and reliability of TACACS+ servers, load balancing also plays a role in optimizing performance. By distributing traffic evenly across multiple servers, load balancing can help prevent individual servers from becoming overloaded and causing delays in processing requests. In high-traffic environments, such as service providers or large enterprises with many network devices, the ability to distribute authentication, authorization, and accounting requests efficiently is critical to maintaining responsiveness. Load balancing helps ensure that all requests are processed in a timely manner, without creating bottlenecks that could delay administrative access to critical devices.

Redundancy is another important benefit of load balancing in TACACS+ deployments. By configuring multiple TACACS+ servers, organizations can ensure that if one server fails, others can continue to handle the authentication and authorization requests. This redundancy is essential for maintaining continuous access control services, particularly in environments where network devices need to be consistently managed by authorized users. Furthermore, the ability to quickly scale the TACACS+ infrastructure by adding additional servers to the load balancing pool ensures that the system can grow with the organization's needs, without experiencing performance degradation or service interruptions.

In conclusion, load balancing is a vital strategy for ensuring the scalability, reliability, and availability of TACACS+ services in large or high-traffic network environments. By distributing traffic across multiple servers, organizations can ensure that their TACACS+ infrastructure can handle high volumes of authentication requests without compromising performance or service availability. Implementing effective load balancing solutions, whether through hardware, software, or DNS-based methods, provides the resilience and flexibility needed to support a robust access control framework. Additionally, session persistence, health monitoring, and redundancy ensure that TACACS+ services remain available and responsive, even in the face of server failures or network disruptions.

TACACS+ and VPN Integration

The integration of TACACS+ with Virtual Private Networks (VPNs) plays a vital role in securing remote access to an organization's internal network. With the growing reliance on remote work and the increasing need for secure connections to corporate resources, VPNs have become a fundamental part of an organization's network security infrastructure. However, simply implementing a VPN solution is not enough to ensure that only authorized users can access the network resources. For this reason, integrating TACACS+ with VPN systems provides an added layer of security by centralizing authentication, authorization, and accounting (AAA) services and ensuring that access control policies are consistently applied, regardless of the user's location.

TACACS+ provides a robust and flexible way to manage user access, as it centralizes the AAA services for network devices, including routers, switches, firewalls, and VPN concentrators. By integrating TACACS+ with VPN systems, organizations can extend these centralized access control mechanisms to remote users, ensuring that VPN connections are secured and authenticated based on organizational policies. The integration enables the use of a single, unified authentication service that supports various remote access methods and devices, streamlining user management and improving security by enforcing consistent access control policies across the entire network infrastructure.

When integrating TACACS+ with a VPN, the TACACS+ server is typically responsible for handling the authentication requests sent by the VPN gateway or VPN concentrator. The VPN gateway acts as a TACACS+ client, forwarding incoming user authentication requests to the TACACS+ server. These requests contain the user's credentials, which may include a username, password, and possibly multi-factor authentication data. The TACACS+ server validates the credentials against its local database or an external identity provider such as Active Directory or LDAP. If the credentials are correct, the TACACS+ server sends an authorization response to the VPN gateway, granting the user access to the network. This process ensures that only authorized users can establish a VPN session and access internal resources.

The benefits of integrating TACACS+ with a VPN system extend beyond simple authentication. One of the key advantages is the ability to enforce granular authorization policies. Once a user is authenticated, TACACS+ can provide the VPN gateway with detailed information about what actions or resources the user is allowed to access. For example, administrators can configure TACACS+ to assign different privilege levels to different user groups, ensuring that only authorized individuals can access sensitive resources. Additionally, TACACS+ can restrict the commands that a user can execute within the VPN session, further controlling the level of access granted.

In organizations where multiple VPN technologies are used, such as SSL VPNs and IPsec VPNs, integrating TACACS+ allows for consistent access policies regardless of the VPN type. Since TACACS+ works with a wide range of network devices, it provides a centralized mechanism for managing user access to various VPN systems. This is particularly useful in large organizations with diverse network architectures, where multiple remote access methods need to be controlled and monitored from a single access control point. By leveraging TACACS+ for both VPN and device authentication, organizations can create a seamless and unified security framework that reduces administrative overhead and improves overall network security.

Another key benefit of integrating TACACS+ with VPN systems is the ability to track and record user activity during VPN sessions. TACACS+ accounting features allow for detailed logging of every user session, including connection times, commands executed, and data accessed. This is particularly valuable for organizations that require compliance with industry regulations such as HIPAA, PCI DSS, or GDPR. The ability to track remote user activity provides a clear audit trail that can be used for compliance reporting, security investigations, and forensic analysis in the event of a breach or other security incident. By maintaining a detailed record of VPN usage, organizations can identify suspicious activities, such as unauthorized access attempts or privilege escalations, and take appropriate action to mitigate potential risks.

The integration of TACACS+ with VPN systems also enhances security by supporting multi-factor authentication (MFA). Multi-factor authentication requires users to provide multiple forms of verification before they can access the network, such as a combination of a password and a one-time token or a biometric factor. TACACS+ can be configured to support MFA, ensuring that users are required to provide multiple pieces of evidence of their identity before being granted access to the VPN. This greatly reduces the risk of unauthorized access due to compromised passwords, as an attacker would need to possess both the password and the second authentication factor. The ability to enforce MFA across VPN sessions strengthens the overall security posture of the organization, especially in environments where sensitive data is being accessed remotely.

When configuring TACACS+ for VPN integration, administrators must ensure that both the VPN gateway and the TACACS+ server are properly configured to handle the authentication and authorization requests. This typically involves configuring the VPN gateway to forward authentication requests to the TACACS+ server using a secure connection, ensuring that communication between the devices is encrypted to prevent data interception. Additionally, administrators must configure the TACACS+ server to handle VPN-specific requests, which may include integrating with external directory services or defining custom policies for remote access. Once the integration is complete, administrators can test the VPN login process to ensure that it functions as expected, with users being properly authenticated and authorized based on the policies defined in TACACS+.

Another consideration when integrating TACACS+ with VPN systems is the management of session timeouts and access expiration. In many cases, organizations need to enforce policies that limit the duration of remote access sessions or automatically disconnect users after a certain period of inactivity. TACACS+ provides administrators with the ability to configure session timeouts and inactivity limits as part of the authorization process. This ensures that users who are no longer active or who have exceeded their allotted session time are automatically logged out, reducing the risk of unauthorized access due to forgotten or abandoned sessions.

The integration of TACACS+ with VPN systems also enables administrators to implement role-based access control (RBAC) for remote users. By assigning users to specific roles, administrators can control the level of access granted to each user based on their role within the organization. For example, a network engineer may have access to advanced VPN commands and configurations, while a remote employee may only have access to basic resources. By using RBAC, organizations can ensure that remote users only have access to the resources they need to perform their job functions, minimizing the risk of data breaches or unauthorized access.

In large-scale environments where multiple VPN servers are deployed across different geographical locations, the integration of TACACS+ allows for centralized management of user access across all VPN systems. This simplifies administrative tasks, as policies can be updated and enforced from a single location, ensuring consistency across the entire network. In addition, the centralized logging and accounting features of TACACS+ provide a unified view of all VPN access activity, making it easier for administrators to monitor usage patterns, identify potential security threats, and comply with regulatory requirements.

Integrating TACACS+ with VPN systems is an essential step in securing remote access to network resources. By providing centralized authentication, authorization, and accounting services, TACACS+ ensures that only authorized users are able to connect to the network, and it enforces consistent security policies across all VPN systems. With the ability to support multi-factor authentication, detailed accounting, and role-based access control, TACACS+ enhances the security and manageability of VPN deployments, making it an invaluable tool for organizations that require secure remote access solutions.

Multi-vendor Device Support with TACACS+

In today's complex network environments, the use of multiple vendors' devices has become a common practice. Whether it's a combination of networking hardware from companies like Cisco, Juniper, Arista, or others, the ability to manage diverse devices efficiently is essential for network administrators. When implementing centralized access control for network devices, TACACS+ (Terminal Access Controller Access-Control System Plus) proves to be an invaluable tool, providing a robust and flexible mechanism for managing authentication, authorization, and accounting (AAA) services across multi-vendor environments. The ability of TACACS+ to support devices from multiple vendors allows organizations to enforce consistent access control policies and streamline user management, regardless of the underlying hardware.

One of the primary strengths of TACACS+ in multi-vendor environments is its vendor-agnostic nature. Unlike proprietary protocols, such as Cisco's RADIUS or vendor-specific access control solutions, TACACS+ is designed to work across a wide range of devices, regardless of the manufacturer. This enables organizations to manage a mixed network infrastructure without the need for separate access control systems for each vendor's devices. TACACS+ standardizes the authentication and authorization process, allowing administrators to enforce consistent security policies and access restrictions across all devices, whether they are from Cisco, Juniper, or another vendor.

In a multi-vendor setup, the integration of TACACS+ simplifies network device management by providing a centralized AAA service. Instead of configuring separate authentication and authorization mechanisms for each type of device, administrators can configure a single TACACS+ server to handle requests from all devices, irrespective of the vendor. This eliminates the need for multiple systems and reduces the complexity of user management. A user's authentication credentials are verified once by the TACACS+ server, and access permissions are granted based on predefined policies, whether the user is accessing a Cisco switch, a Juniper router, or any other device supported by TACACS+.

Another advantage of using TACACS+ in multi-vendor environments is its flexibility in handling different command sets and privilege levels. Each vendor's devices often have their own set of commands for configuration, management, and troubleshooting, and these commands can differ significantly between vendors. TACACS+ addresses this challenge by allowing administrators to define detailed command authorization policies for each device type. This flexibility ensures that, regardless of the vendor, only authorized commands are executed by users. For example, a user with administrative privileges may be allowed to execute configuration commands on a Cisco router but be restricted from making changes on a Juniper firewall. TACACS+ provides the necessary tools to manage such granular command-level access, enhancing security by preventing unauthorized or potentially harmful actions.

In addition to command-level authorization, TACACS+ supports the use of privilege levels, which define the degree of access granted to users on network devices. Privilege levels are an important aspect of multi-vendor support, as different vendors may use different privilege level systems. TACACS+ standardizes this process, allowing administrators to map privilege levels across various devices into a consistent access control framework. For instance, a user might have a privilege level of 15 on a Cisco device, which grants full administrative access, while on a Juniper device, the same user might only be assigned a privilege level of 5, which limits them to view-only access. This consistency helps network administrators enforce the principle of least privilege across their infrastructure, ensuring that users only have access to the resources they need to perform their jobs.

TACACS+ also supports the use of external identity sources, such as LDAP or Active Directory, in multi-vendor environments. In large organizations with diverse network devices from various vendors, managing user identities across multiple platforms can be cumbersome. However, by integrating TACACS+ with LDAP or Active Directory, administrators can centralize user authentication and manage user access based on their roles or group memberships in the directory. This integration allows for easier management of user accounts and reduces the administrative overhead associated with maintaining separate user databases for each vendor's devices. Furthermore, it enhances security by ensuring that user credentials are stored and managed in a centralized and secure directory, reducing the risk of credential leakage or mismanagement.

Accounting is another critical feature of TACACS+ that benefits multi-vendor environments. TACACS+ provides detailed logs of user activities, including login attempts, command executions, and session durations. These logs are essential for auditing purposes, troubleshooting, and compliance with regulatory standards. In multi-vendor environments, where devices from different manufacturers may have different logging formats and structures, TACACS+ standardizes the accounting process, ensuring that all activities are logged in a consistent format, regardless of the device vendor. This uniformity simplifies the process of monitoring network access, analyzing user behavior, and investigating security incidents across the entire network, making it easier for administrators to maintain a clear record of who accessed what devices and when.

Security is a primary concern in multi-vendor networks, and TACACS+ plays a crucial role in ensuring that access to network devices is tightly controlled. Since TACACS+ encrypts the entire communication between the client and server, all sensitive information, including passwords, command data, and session details, is protected from interception and tampering. This encryption is especially important in multi-vendor environments, where devices may be distributed across different physical locations or connected over less-secure networks. By securing the communication channels, TACACS+ mitigates the risk of man-in-the-middle attacks, eavesdropping, or data corruption, ensuring that only authorized users can access and manage network devices.

In multi-vendor environments, interoperability can sometimes be a challenge. However, TACACS+ is widely supported by a diverse range of networking hardware, which makes it a reliable choice for organizations with heterogeneous network infrastructures. By using TACACS+ as the centralized AAA solution, organizations can ensure that all devices, regardless of their vendor, are governed by the same set of access control policies, making network management simpler and more secure. Whether the network includes routers, switches, firewalls, or wireless access points from different manufacturers, TACACS+ enables seamless integration and consistent policy enforcement across all devices.

The use of TACACS+ in multi-vendor environments not only simplifies network management but also provides a level of security and flexibility that is difficult to achieve with vendor-specific solutions. By centralizing authentication, authorization, and accounting services, TACACS+ enables organizations to enforce uniform security policies across a diverse range of network devices, regardless of the manufacturer. Its ability to manage command-level access, support various privilege levels, and integrate with external identity sources makes it a powerful tool for ensuring that network access is both secure and efficient. With TACACS+, organizations can maintain strict control over user activities, enhance security, and reduce the complexity of managing multi-vendor network infrastructures.

Scripting and Automation with TACACS

TACACS, or Terminal Access Controller Access-Control System, is a protocol commonly used in networking environments for managing access to network devices. It is a key component in ensuring secure authentication, authorization, and accounting (AAA) for devices such as routers, switches, and firewalls. While TACACS provides robust security and control, many network administrators find that the protocol's functionality can be further enhanced through scripting and automation. By leveraging these techniques, network administrators can simplify the management of access controls, improve network efficiency, and ensure consistent security configurations across large and complex environments. Scripting and automation provide an effective means of streamlining the management of TACACS, particularly in large-scale environments where manual configurations would be time-consuming and prone to error.

The primary benefit of incorporating scripting and automation into the management of TACACS is the ability to centralize and standardize access controls. In a typical network setup, administrators are often required to configure access policies for a range of devices. Without automation, this process requires manual intervention, which increases the likelihood of inconsistencies or mistakes. By automating TACACS configurations, administrators can ensure that each device is configured in a standardized way, reducing the chances of errors and simplifying future management tasks. Scripts can be written to handle tasks such as creating or modifying TACACS policies, configuring user groups, and specifying device access levels. With the right scripts in place, administrators can ensure that all devices are compliant with organizational security policies, which helps mitigate the risk of unauthorized access or configuration errors.

In addition to reducing the administrative burden, scripting and automation also improve the scalability of TACACS-based environments. As networks grow, the number of devices that need to be configured and managed increases significantly. Manually configuring each device is not only inefficient but also impractical, especially for large enterprises with thousands of network devices. Automation allows network administrators to apply consistent configurations across all devices at once, making it easier to scale the network infrastructure. By utilizing scripts, it is possible to automate tasks such as user provisioning, policy enforcement, and logging, ensuring that as new devices are added to the network, they are automatically configured with the correct TACACS settings. This level of automation also makes it easier to roll out changes across the network, whether it involves updating authentication policies, adding new user groups, or making security updates.

Another advantage of scripting and automation with TACACS is the ability to integrate the protocol with other network management tools and systems. In modern networking environments, administrators often rely on a variety of tools to monitor and manage network performance, security, and device configurations. By using scripts, TACACS can be seamlessly integrated with these systems to provide a more comprehensive solution. For instance, scripts can be written to synchronize TACACS configurations with network monitoring systems, ensuring that the authentication and access policies are consistently aligned with overall network policies. This integration can help improve the visibility of network activity, enabling administrators to quickly identify potential security issues or unauthorized access attempts. Furthermore, automation can be used to streamline the process of updating TACACS configurations in response to changes in network infrastructure, such as adding or removing devices or modifying access policies.

The use of scripting in TACACS management also enhances troubleshooting capabilities. In a complex network environment, issues can arise that may affect the performance or functionality of TACACS, such as connectivity problems, misconfigured policies, or unauthorized access attempts. By utilizing scripts to automate diagnostic tasks, administrators can quickly identify and resolve issues without having to manually check each device or configuration. For example, scripts can be written to check the status of TACACS servers, verify the integrity of access policies, and perform routine system checks. In the event of an issue, these scripts can be used to pinpoint the source of the problem and automatically apply corrective actions, such as reloading configurations or restarting affected devices. This level of automation not only improves troubleshooting efficiency but also reduces downtime and ensures that the network remains secure and operational.

Moreover, automation plays a critical role in improving compliance and auditing within TACACS-managed environments. Regulatory requirements and internal security policies often mandate that network devices adhere to specific security configurations. Manually ensuring compliance across a large network can be a daunting task, particularly when dealing with multiple devices and changing requirements. Scripting and automation can simplify this process by continuously monitoring configurations and ensuring that all devices remain compliant with established security standards. Scripts can be set up to regularly check the configurations of network devices and compare them against predefined security baselines. If any discrepancies are found, the automation system can trigger alerts or even make automatic adjustments to bring the devices back into compliance. This reduces the administrative effort required to manage compliance and helps ensure that security standards are consistently met.

Furthermore, scripting and automation provide greater flexibility and control over TACACS configurations. Administrators can create custom scripts tailored to the specific needs of their network environment, enabling them to automate tasks that are unique to their infrastructure. For example, scripts can be designed to handle complex user roles and access levels, ensuring that different users are granted the appropriate permissions based on their job functions or departments. Additionally, automation can be used to enforce dynamic access policies, such as adjusting access levels based on time of day or network conditions. This level of flexibility allows network administrators to implement more granular and adaptive security controls, ensuring that access is always appropriately restricted based on the context and requirements of the network.

In conclusion, the integration of scripting and automation with TACACS offers significant advantages for network administrators. It allows for the centralization and standardization of access policies, improves scalability, and enhances the integration with other network management tools. By automating routine tasks and troubleshooting processes, administrators can save time and resources while ensuring that the network remains secure and compliant with security policies. As network environments continue to grow in size and complexity, the role of scripting and automation in managing TACACS will become increasingly important in maintaining efficient, secure, and compliant access control systems across large-scale networks.

Using TACACS with Network Access Control (NAC) Solutions

Network Access Control (NAC) solutions are crucial for ensuring that only authorized devices and users can access a network. They play an essential role in enforcing security policies and providing visibility into network activity. One of the most effective ways to enhance the security and manageability of NAC systems is by integrating them with TACACS, or Terminal Access Controller Access-Control System. TACACS is a protocol used primarily for managing authentication, authorization, and accounting (AAA) of network devices. By combining TACACS with NAC solutions, organizations can streamline access control processes, improve security, and ensure a consistent, high level of protection across the entire network.

The integration of TACACS with NAC solutions allows network administrators to create a more comprehensive and robust security framework. NAC solutions are designed to evaluate devices attempting to connect to the network based on various factors such as compliance with security policies, device health, and the user's credentials. However, while NAC solutions handle device authentication and access control, they often rely on additional protocols like TACACS to provide granular control over device-specific access privileges. By using TACACS, network administrators can define and enforce more detailed access policies that govern which users can access specific devices and what actions they can perform once authenticated. This combination of NAC and TACACS ensures that devices are not only authorized to connect but also have access to the right resources in line with organizational policies.

In addition to providing enhanced control, the use of TACACS with NAC solutions strengthens security by ensuring that all access attempts are properly authenticated and authorized. TACACS, as a protocol, offers more flexibility than other alternatives like RADIUS, particularly when it comes to managing device-specific access privileges. With TACACS, administrators can define specific permissions for different users and devices, ensuring that access rights are granted on a per-device and per-user basis. This is critical for organizations with diverse network infrastructures, where different devices may require different levels of access depending on their function. For instance, network administrators may need to restrict certain users from configuring routers but grant them full access to switches or firewalls. By integrating TACACS with NAC, administrators can enforce these fine-grained policies more efficiently, ensuring a high level of security across the network.

Moreover, combining TACACS with NAC provides better visibility and auditing capabilities. TACACS can log detailed information about user access attempts, including who accessed a device, when they accessed it, and what actions they performed. This audit trail is crucial for compliance with various industry regulations, such as HIPAA or PCI-DSS, which require organizations to maintain detailed logs of user activities. When integrated with NAC systems, TACACS can offer a centralized view of network access activities, providing administrators with insights into who is accessing which devices and whether those accesses are legitimate. This centralized approach not only simplifies the monitoring and auditing processes but also enhances the overall security posture of the organization by enabling administrators to quickly identify any unauthorized access attempts or suspicious activities.

Furthermore, the use of TACACS with NAC solutions enables more efficient user management and policy enforcement. NAC solutions are typically used to ensure that devices meet certain health and security criteria before they are allowed to access the network. However, these solutions often need to be paired with a method of managing user access once the device is connected. TACACS serves this role by allowing administrators to assign specific access rights based on user credentials and roles. This integration ensures that once a device is authenticated and granted network access by the NAC solution, the user's role and permissions are immediately enforced by TACACS, ensuring consistent policy enforcement across all network devices. This is particularly useful in environments where users may move between devices or locations, as TACACS can provide a consistent experience and ensure that users only have access to the resources they are authorized to use.

The integration of TACACS with NAC also improves the overall scalability and flexibility of network access control systems. As organizations grow and their network infrastructures become more complex, the need to manage access to an increasing number of devices and users grows as well. With TACACS handling the granular authentication and authorization processes, administrators can ensure that new devices and users are automatically integrated into the network with the appropriate access rights. Additionally, because TACACS is a highly customizable protocol, it can be tailored to meet the unique needs of any network environment. Whether the organization has a small, single-site network or a large, multi-site deployment, the combination of TACACS with NAC ensures that access control remains consistent and scalable, even as the network expands.

One of the most significant benefits of integrating TACACS with NAC is the enhanced ability to enforce dynamic access policies. NAC solutions often use real-time assessments to determine whether a device is compliant with security policies before granting network access. This can include checking for the latest antivirus definitions, ensuring that operating systems are up to date, and verifying that the device is not compromised. Once a device passes these assessments, the NAC solution typically grants access to the network, but the level of access is often determined by TACACS. TACACS allows for the enforcement of dynamic policies that can adapt based on the security posture of the device. For example, if a device is found to be running outdated software or missing critical security patches, TACACS can limit its access to sensitive resources until the issue is resolved, ensuring that only fully compliant devices have access to critical parts of the network.

In environments where security is a top priority, the combination of TACACS and NAC offers a higher level of protection against unauthorized access. By leveraging TACACS for device-specific authentication and authorization, administrators can ensure that access to network devices is strictly controlled and monitored. Additionally, the granular control provided by TACACS allows for more sophisticated policies that can be enforced based on the specific requirements of the organization. For example, administrators can implement time-based access policies, restrict access to certain devices based on user roles, or even enforce two-factor authentication for certain actions. These advanced security features help ensure that only authorized users can access critical network devices and perform sensitive operations, reducing the likelihood of security breaches or unauthorized configurations.

The combination of TACACS and NAC also facilitates smoother device lifecycle management. As devices are added to or removed from the network, TACACS can automatically enforce the necessary access policies, ensuring that new devices are properly authenticated and authorized to join the network. Similarly, when devices are decommissioned or removed from the network, TACACS can revoke their access, ensuring that they no longer have network privileges. This level of automation simplifies the process of managing device access and ensures that security is maintained throughout the lifecycle of each device.

Integrating TACACS with NAC solutions ultimately strengthens the overall security infrastructure of an organization by providing a unified and flexible approach to network access control. With TACACS handling the authentication, authorization, and accounting processes, and NAC solutions ensuring that only compliant devices are allowed to access the network, organizations can maintain a secure and well-managed network environment. This combination of technologies not only improves the efficiency of network management but also enhances the security and compliance of the network, providing a comprehensive solution for managing network access in today's increasingly complex IT environments.

Zero Trust Architecture and TACACS

Zero Trust Architecture (ZTA) is an evolving security framework that has gained significant traction in recent years. The core principle of Zero Trust is based on the idea that trust should never be implicitly granted, regardless of the user's location, device, or network. In this model, all network traffic is considered untrusted, and verification is required for every access attempt, whether from inside or outside the network perimeter. The Zero Trust model operates on the principle of least privilege, ensuring that users, devices, and applications only have access to the resources they need to perform their tasks. In this environment, access controls are implemented rigorously, and security is constantly enforced, leaving no room for trust by default. The integration of TACACS (Terminal Access Controller Access-Control System) with Zero Trust Architecture offers a comprehensive solution to managing authentication, authorization, and accounting (AAA) in a Zero Trust network, providing granular control over access to network devices and services.

One of the primary challenges of implementing a Zero Trust model is the effective management of authentication and authorization across a diverse and often distributed network environment. In traditional network models, security measures typically focus on perimeter defense, where once a user or device is inside the network, they are trusted. However, in a Zero Trust model, there is no implicit trust for any user or device, meaning that every request for access must be authenticated, authorized, and continuously monitored. TACACS, as a protocol designed to centralize and manage authentication, authorization, and accounting for network devices, plays a vital role in this model by ensuring that access control is robust and consistent. When integrated with a Zero Trust network, TACACS helps enforce the strict security policies required by the model, ensuring that only authorized users and devices can interact with network resources.

The use of TACACS in a Zero Trust environment provides administrators with detailed control over user access to network devices. TACACS is known for its ability to offer fine-grained control over who can access a particular device, what actions they can perform once logged in, and how their actions are logged for auditing purposes. In a Zero Trust framework, this level of control is crucial because it ensures that network devices, such as routers, switches, and firewalls, are only accessible by authenticated users who meet specific criteria. For instance, TACACS can enforce policies that restrict certain users to only read access or limit their ability to make configuration changes, ensuring that network devices are protected from unauthorized or malicious activity. This integration enables administrators to apply the principle of least privilege at the device level, which is a cornerstone of Zero Trust security.

Another significant benefit of using TACACS within a Zero Trust model is its ability to maintain a centralized and consistent approach to access control. In a traditional network setup, managing access controls can be a challenging and fragmented task, especially in large, distributed environments. Devices may be spread across multiple locations, and ensuring consistent access control policies across all devices can become complex. TACACS addresses this challenge by centralizing access management, providing a unified system for controlling who can access network devices and what actions they are permitted to perform. This centralized approach ensures that the same stringent security policies are applied consistently across all devices in the network, whether they are located on-site or remotely. By using TACACS, administrators can create a cohesive security framework that aligns with Zero Trust principles, ensuring that access to all devices is continuously monitored and controlled.

In a Zero Trust environment, every user, device, and application is treated as potentially compromised until proven otherwise. This requires continuous monitoring and verification of all access attempts. TACACS plays a crucial role in this process by enabling administrators to enforce multi-factor authentication (MFA) and monitor all user activity in real time. By integrating TACACS with a Zero Trust network, administrators can require additional authentication steps for users attempting to access network devices, ensuring that access is not only contingent upon valid credentials but also on the real-time assessment of the user's identity. For instance, users may be required to provide a second form of authentication, such as a one-time password or biometric verification, before being granted access to sensitive devices. This added layer of security is essential in a Zero Trust model, where the emphasis is on verifying every user and device interaction before granting access.

Furthermore, the continuous monitoring and auditing capabilities provided by TACACS complement the Zero Trust model's emphasis on vigilance and real-time security. TACACS generates detailed logs of all user activities, including login attempts, executed commands, and changes made to device configurations. These logs serve as an invaluable resource for network administrators in maintaining visibility into network activity and ensuring that security policies are being adhered to. In a Zero Trust network, where every action is scrutinized and every access attempt is recorded, the ability to track and analyze these logs is critical for detecting and responding to potential security threats. Administrators can use these logs to identify unusual patterns of behavior, such as unauthorized access attempts or attempts to bypass security controls, and take immediate action to mitigate any risks.

As the Zero Trust model expands beyond traditional network perimeters, organizations often face the challenge of securing access to cloud-based resources, mobile devices, and remote workers. In this distributed and dynamic environment, TACACS provides a reliable method of enforcing consistent access control policies across all devices, regardless of their location. Whether an employee is working from home, accessing cloud resources, or connecting to the network through a VPN, TACACS ensures that access is governed by the same rigorous authentication and authorization procedures. By integrating TACACS with cloud-based NAC solutions, organizations can extend the Zero Trust principles to their cloud infrastructure, ensuring that every device, regardless of its origin, is subjected to the same stringent security policies. This approach helps organizations manage the complexities of modern, hybrid environments, ensuring that access control remains consistent and secure across all entry points to the network.

One of the key challenges of implementing Zero Trust is the ability to dynamically adapt to changing network conditions and security threats. As threats evolve and new vulnerabilities are discovered, it is essential that access control systems can be quickly updated to address emerging risks. TACACS provides the flexibility needed to respond to these changes by allowing administrators to easily modify access policies and user privileges. For example, if a new vulnerability is identified in a specific device or application, administrators can use TACACS to quickly revoke or modify user access to that device until the issue is resolved. This dynamic approach to access control ensures that security is not static but continuously adapts to the evolving threat landscape, which is a fundamental requirement of the Zero Trust model.

The integration of TACACS with Zero Trust Architecture represents a powerful combination of technologies that can provide organizations with a robust, scalable, and flexible security framework. TACACS enhances the Zero Trust model by providing fine-grained control over access to network devices, ensuring that only authorized users and devices are granted access. It also supports multi-factor authentication, continuous monitoring, and detailed auditing, all of which are essential components of a Zero Trust network. As organizations continue to adopt Zero Trust principles to secure their networks, the use of TACACS as a central element of their access control strategy will be critical to ensuring that access to sensitive resources is tightly controlled and continuously monitored, providing a higher level of security and compliance across all areas of the network.

Best Practices for TACACS Policy Design

When designing TACACS (Terminal Access Controller Access-Control System) policies, network administrators need to prioritize security, scalability, and manageability. TACACS is a protocol used for managing authentication, authorization, and accounting (AAA) within a network, and it plays a critical role in controlling access to network devices, ensuring that only authorized users are granted appropriate privileges. A well-structured TACACS policy ensures that access to sensitive resources is protected, reduces the risk of unauthorized access, and provides a clear audit trail for accountability. Designing effective TACACS policies involves several considerations, each contributing to the overall strength and efficiency of network access control. Adhering to best practices when designing TACACS policies is crucial for maintaining a secure and compliant network environment.

One of the foundational best practices in TACACS policy design is the principle of least privilege. This principle dictates that users should only be granted the minimum level of access necessary for them to perform their tasks. When designing TACACS policies, administrators should avoid granting broad, unrestricted access to network devices, instead tailoring access controls based on specific roles, responsibilities, and job functions. For example, network engineers may need full access to modify device configurations, while network support staff may only need read-only access to monitor network performance. By defining granular roles and permissions for different user groups, administrators can ensure that users have access only to the resources they need, which helps reduce the potential attack surface within the network.

Another important best practice when designing TACACS policies is to ensure that authentication methods are strong and secure. While TACACS supports several authentication mechanisms, it is essential to configure the system to require strong authentication methods to protect against unauthorized access. The use of multi-factor authentication (MFA) is highly recommended in TACACS implementations, as it adds an additional layer of security. MFA requires users to provide multiple forms of verification, such as something they know (password), something they have (token or smart card), or something they are (biometric data). By integrating MFA with TACACS, administrators can significantly increase the security of network device access, making it more difficult for attackers to gain unauthorized access, even if they have compromised a user's password.

Scalability is another critical consideration when designing TACACS policies. As networks grow in size and complexity, the number of devices and users that need to be managed also increases. To accommodate this growth, TACACS policies should be designed with scalability in mind. One effective approach is to use hierarchical structures for user groups and device access policies. By creating a well-organized structure of user groups, administrators can easily assign permissions to users based on their role within the organization, rather than configuring access controls individually for each user. This structure can be extended to include device-specific policies, ensuring that access to different types of network devices is appropriately controlled. For example, administrators may want to apply different policies to routers, switches, and firewalls based on their level of sensitivity and the specific tasks each device supports.

An essential aspect of TACACS policy design is the implementation of strong auditing and logging mechanisms. TACACS provides the ability to log detailed information about user access attempts, including login times, actions performed, and any configuration changes made to network devices. This logging capability is vital for maintaining accountability and ensuring that all access attempts are properly monitored. When designing TACACS policies, administrators should ensure that logging is enabled for all devices and that logs are stored securely for later review. The logs should capture enough detail to provide insight into who accessed what resources and when, as well as what actions were taken during each session. Additionally, it is important to implement a retention policy for logs, ensuring that they are kept for an appropriate period to comply with regulatory requirements and for security auditing purposes.

Segmentation of network access is another best practice in TACACS policy design. Segmenting access based on user roles, departments, or device types can help prevent unauthorized access and reduce the potential impact of a security breach. For example, users in the finance department may require different access privileges than users in the marketing department, and network administrators may need more extensive access to network devices than end users. By segmenting access in this way, administrators can better manage access control and reduce the risk of privilege escalation or lateral movement in the event of a compromise. Additionally, segmentation can help ensure that sensitive resources, such as financial data or customer information, are only accessible to users who have a legitimate need to access them.

When designing TACACS policies, it is also crucial to ensure that access controls are enforced consistently across the network. This consistency is important for maintaining security and simplifying network management. Administrators should avoid creating exceptions or ad-hoc configurations that can lead to inconsistencies in access control. Instead, they should implement standardized policies that apply uniformly to all devices and users. This approach not only simplifies the configuration process but also ensures that security policies are applied consistently, making it easier to detect and address any discrepancies or vulnerabilities.

Regular review and updating of TACACS policies are also essential for maintaining a secure network environment. As the network evolves and new devices are added, existing policies should be reviewed to ensure that they remain relevant and effective. Additionally, changes in organizational structure, business processes, or regulatory requirements may necessitate updates to access controls. Periodically auditing TACACS policies can help identify potential gaps in security and provide an opportunity to refine access control mechanisms. By keeping TACACS policies up to date, administrators can ensure that security measures remain aligned with the organization's needs and the evolving threat landscape.

Another key consideration when designing TACACS policies is ensuring that policies are aligned with industry standards and regulatory requirements. Many industries, such as healthcare, finance, and government, have specific regulations regarding access control and data security. When designing TACACS policies, administrators should familiarize themselves with the relevant regulations that apply to their organization and ensure that the policies they create comply with these standards. This may involve implementing specific access controls, such as restricting access to sensitive data or requiring certain types of authentication. By aligning TACACS policies with regulatory requirements, administrators can help ensure that the organization remains compliant and avoids potential legal and financial penalties.

In addition to these considerations, it is important to provide training and documentation for users and administrators who interact with the TACACS system. Ensuring that users understand the access policies and are aware of their responsibilities can help prevent inadvertent violations of security protocols. Similarly, administrators should be provided with the necessary tools and resources to effectively manage and monitor TACACS configurations. Comprehensive documentation of the TACACS policy design and configuration process is also essential for troubleshooting, auditing, and future policy modifications.

Finally, testing and validation of TACACS policies are critical to ensuring that they work as intended. Before deploying a new policy or making changes to an existing one, administrators should thoroughly test the policy in a controlled environment to ensure that it does not inadvertently grant excessive privileges or block legitimate access. This testing process can help identify any potential issues before they impact the production network, ensuring that TACACS policies are both secure and effective.

Designing effective TACACS policies is a vital part of managing network security and ensuring that only authorized users can access sensitive resources. By adhering to best practices such as the principle of least privilege, implementing strong authentication methods, ensuring scalability, enabling auditing and logging, and regularly reviewing and updating policies, administrators can create a robust TACACS policy framework that provides comprehensive access control, enhances security, and ensures compliance with industry standards.

Incident Response and TACACS Logs

In modern network environments, security incidents can happen at any time. The need for rapid identification, containment, and resolution of such incidents is paramount in minimizing potential damage and maintaining the integrity of the organization's infrastructure. A key component of this process is the use of logs to track user activity and system changes. TACACS (Terminal Access Controller Access-Control System), as a protocol for managing authentication, authorization, and accounting (AAA) of network devices, plays a critical role in this aspect. TACACS logs contain valuable information that can help network administrators respond to incidents effectively, investigate suspicious activity, and ensure compliance with security policies. Understanding how to secure and manage these logs is essential for maintaining a strong security posture and ensuring the smooth functioning of incident response processes.

TACACS logs contain detailed records of user access to network devices, including login attempts, executed commands, and changes made to configurations. These logs provide essential visibility into who accessed what resources and what actions were taken, which is critical for incident detection and forensic analysis. In the event of a security incident, TACACS logs can help administrators identify the source of the breach, the methods used by the attacker, and the actions taken during the attack. For example, if an unauthorized user gains access to a network device, the TACACS logs can provide information about the time of access, the user's credentials, and any actions performed during the session. This data can be instrumental in understanding the scope of the attack and determining the appropriate response.

One of the most important steps in incident response is ensuring that TACACS logs are secure and protected from unauthorized access. These logs contain sensitive information that could be used by attackers to gain further access to network resources. If an attacker gains access to the TACACS logs, they could potentially identify weaknesses in the authentication or authorization processes, or even gain insight into the specific commands that were executed during previous sessions. To prevent this, TACACS logs should be stored in a secure location with limited access. This can be achieved by using centralized log management systems that provide strong access controls and encryption to protect the logs from tampering or unauthorized access.

In addition to securing the physical storage of TACACS logs, it is also essential to ensure that the logs are transmitted securely. During the incident response process, logs may need to be transmitted between systems for analysis or correlation. Without proper encryption, this transmission could be intercepted by attackers, potentially exposing sensitive information. To prevent this, TACACS logs should be transmitted over secure channels, such as SSL/TLS, which encrypt the data during transmission. By securing the transmission of logs, organizations can ensure that the integrity of the logs is maintained and that sensitive information is not exposed during the incident response process.

Another key aspect of securing TACACS logs is ensuring their integrity. Logs can be tampered with by attackers to cover their tracks or erase evidence of malicious activity. To prevent this, organizations should implement logging mechanisms that protect the integrity of the logs and detect any tampering attempts. This can include using cryptographic hashes or digital signatures to verify the integrity of logs, ensuring that any modifications made to the logs are detectable. Additionally, organizations should configure their log management systems to generate alerts in the event of suspicious activity, such as log deletion or modification. This provides administrators with real-time visibility into potential tampering and enables them to respond quickly to secure the logs and investigate the incident.

As part of an incident response plan, organizations should also define retention policies for TACACS logs. Retention policies specify how long logs should be kept before being archived or deleted. These policies are critical for ensuring that logs are available for analysis during an incident and that they comply with regulatory requirements. In many industries, regulatory frameworks such as GDPR or PCI-DSS mandate that logs be retained for a specific period. Failing to maintain the proper retention schedule can result in non-compliance and hinder the organization's ability to investigate incidents effectively. By defining and adhering to retention policies, organizations can ensure that TACACS logs are available when needed and that they meet legal and regulatory requirements.

When an incident occurs, the logs generated by TACACS can be invaluable for forensic analysis. By reviewing TACACS logs, administrators can reconstruct the sequence of events leading up to the incident, identify any vulnerabilities that were exploited, and determine the scope of the attack. This information can be used to improve security defenses and prevent similar incidents in the future. For example, if a vulnerability in the TACACS authentication process is identified during an incident, administrators can take steps to patch the vulnerability and prevent future attacks. Additionally, the logs can provide evidence that can be used in legal proceedings or to meet reporting requirements for regulatory bodies.

The ability to correlate TACACS logs with other logs in the network is another critical aspect of incident response. Many security incidents involve multiple systems and devices, and the ability to correlate logs from different sources can provide a more complete picture of the incident. By integrating TACACS logs with other logging systems, such as those that track network traffic or system events, administrators can gain greater visibility into the attack and identify any related incidents. This correlation can help detect advanced persistent threats (APTs) and other sophisticated attacks that may involve multiple steps and systems. By leveraging the full range of log data, organizations can improve their ability to detect, respond to, and mitigate incidents.

In addition to incident response, TACACS logs also play an important role in ongoing security monitoring. Regularly reviewing and analyzing TACACS logs as part of a continuous monitoring strategy can help administrators identify potential security threats before they escalate into full-blown incidents. For example, repeated failed login attempts or unusual login patterns may indicate that an attacker is attempting to brute force credentials. By monitoring TACACS logs for these types of events, administrators can take proactive measures to block unauthorized access and prevent potential breaches. Continuous monitoring of TACACS logs also helps ensure that security policies are being adhered to and that access controls are functioning as intended.

TACACS logs also provide valuable insight into compliance with security standards and regulatory requirements. Many organizations must adhere to strict regulatory frameworks that require detailed records of access to sensitive systems and devices. By maintaining secure TACACS logs, organizations can demonstrate compliance with these regulations and provide auditors with the necessary documentation to verify that proper access controls are in place. Additionally, secure logging practices help organizations meet industry-specific requirements, such as those outlined by HIPAA for healthcare organizations or PCI-DSS for organizations that process credit card transactions.

In the context of incident response, secure and well-managed TACACS logs provide a crucial source of information that can be used to detect, investigate, and respond to security incidents. By ensuring that these logs are properly secured, transmitted, and stored, organizations can maintain the integrity of their log data and use it to effectively respond to incidents and protect their networks. TACACS logs provide a detailed record of user activity and system changes, offering administrators the insights they need to investigate incidents, improve security, and ensure compliance. Properly managing these logs is not just a best practice but a vital component of an organization's overall security strategy.

Integrating TACACS with SIEM Systems

In the realm of network security, integration between different security systems is crucial for providing a comprehensive and unified approach to threat detection and response. One such integration that can significantly enhance the security posture of an organization is the integration of TACACS (Terminal Access Controller Access-Control System) with SIEM (Security Information and Event Management) systems. TACACS is a protocol that manages authentication, authorization, and accounting (AAA) for network devices, while SIEM systems are designed to collect, analyze, and correlate security data from various sources across the network to detect potential threats and ensure compliance. By integrating TACACS with SIEM systems, organizations can leverage the detailed logs provided by TACACS to gain deeper insights into user activity, identify suspicious behavior, and respond more effectively to security incidents. This integration allows for more centralized and automated security monitoring, improving both the efficiency and accuracy of threat detection.

One of the primary benefits of integrating TACACS with SIEM systems is the ability to correlate network device access logs with other security events across the organization. TACACS logs contain valuable information regarding user access to network devices, including login attempts, command executions, and changes made to device configurations. By feeding this data into a SIEM system, security analysts can correlate this access information with other logs from firewalls, intrusion detection systems, or endpoints, creating a more comprehensive view of potential security incidents. For example, if an unauthorized user attempts to access a router using a compromised account, the SIEM system can correlate this event with other suspicious activities, such as unusual traffic patterns or access attempts on other devices, helping security teams to detect the attack and respond quickly. This correlation capability is especially important in identifying advanced threats that span multiple network layers or devices, as it provides a broader context for analysis and detection.

Another advantage of integrating TACACS with SIEM systems is the ability to automate alerting and incident response. SIEM systems are designed to process vast amounts of log data in real time, enabling them to identify patterns and anomalies that may indicate a security incident. By integrating TACACS logs into the SIEM system, organizations can configure automated alerts for specific events, such as failed login attempts, excessive privilege escalations, or unauthorized changes to network device configurations. For example, if a user with a limited role attempts to make unauthorized changes to a critical network device, the SIEM system can trigger an alert, notifying security personnel of a potential security breach. This automated alerting helps to ensure that security incidents are detected and addressed promptly, reducing the time between detection and response and minimizing the potential impact of the attack.

The integration of TACACS with SIEM systems also enhances compliance management and auditing capabilities. Many organizations are required to meet regulatory standards such as HIPAA, PCI-DSS, or SOX, which mandate strict control and monitoring of access to sensitive network resources. TACACS, by providing detailed logs of user access and actions on network devices, plays a critical role in fulfilling these compliance requirements. When these TACACS logs are integrated with a SIEM system, organizations can easily generate compliance reports and track user activity across the network. The SIEM system can automate the process of collecting, storing, and analyzing these logs, ensuring that they are readily available for audit purposes. This integration not only simplifies compliance efforts but also provides a more accurate and comprehensive audit trail, which is essential in demonstrating adherence to regulatory requirements and identifying any deviations from standard security practices.

In addition to improving compliance and monitoring, the integration of TACACS with SIEM systems also facilitates more proactive security measures. TACACS logs, when integrated with a SIEM system, provide security analysts with rich data that can be used for threat hunting and identifying vulnerabilities before they are exploited. For instance, security analysts can use the combined data from TACACS and other sources to search for indicators of compromise, such as unusual login times or repeated failed authentication attempts, that may indicate an ongoing attack. This proactive approach allows security teams to identify potential threats before they escalate into full-blown incidents, enabling them to mitigate risks early in the attack lifecycle. By continuously monitoring TACACS logs alongside other security data, SIEM systems provide a comprehensive view of the network's security posture, helping to identify areas of vulnerability that may need to be addressed.

Moreover, integrating TACACS with SIEM systems strengthens the ability to perform forensic analysis after a security incident has occurred. When a security breach happens, it is crucial to understand how the attacker gained access, what actions were taken, and what devices or systems were affected. TACACS logs provide a detailed record of user activity on network devices, which can be invaluable in reconstructing the sequence of events during a breach. When these logs are integrated with a SIEM system, investigators can correlate TACACS data with other relevant logs, such as firewall or IDS logs, to piece together the full story of the attack. This level of visibility into the attacker's movements allows security teams to understand the scope of the breach, identify any compromised systems, and implement necessary measures to prevent similar attacks in the future. Additionally, the SIEM system can generate detailed reports that document the timeline of events and provide a clear audit trail, which is essential for legal or regulatory purposes.

Furthermore, the integration of TACACS with SIEM systems contributes to more efficient and effective incident response. When a security event occurs, having all relevant data in one centralized location makes it easier for security teams to assess the situation and take appropriate action. By integrating TACACS logs with SIEM, security personnel can quickly access information about who attempted to log in, what commands were executed, and which devices were affected, allowing them to make more informed decisions. This streamlined access to data can significantly speed up the investigation and response process, helping organizations contain and mitigate the impact of security incidents more efficiently. Additionally, the SIEM system can automate certain aspects of incident response, such as blocking suspicious IP addresses or disabling compromised accounts, further improving response times and minimizing damage.

The integration of TACACS with SIEM systems also facilitates better communication and collaboration between security teams. By centralizing all security logs and alerts in a single platform, SIEM systems enable security analysts, incident responders, and compliance officers to work together more effectively. TACACS logs, along with other network security data, can be easily shared among team members, ensuring that everyone has access to the same information and can collaborate on identifying and resolving security issues. This centralized approach helps to break down silos within the organization, promoting a more cohesive and coordinated response to security threats.

In summary, integrating TACACS with SIEM systems offers numerous benefits for organizations seeking to enhance their security posture and improve their incident response capabilities. By correlating TACACS logs with other security data, organizations can gain a comprehensive view of their network activity, enabling them to detect and respond to threats more effectively. The integration also streamlines compliance management, improves forensic analysis, and enhances incident response efficiency. With the growing complexity and sophistication of cyber threats, the integration of TACACS with SIEM systems is becoming an essential practice for organizations that want to stay ahead of potential security risks and ensure the safety of their network resources.

Advanced Use Cases: Multi-Factor Authentication

Multi-factor authentication (MFA) is increasingly recognized as a critical component of modern security frameworks. As cyber threats continue to grow more sophisticated, the need for stronger authentication mechanisms has become apparent. MFA significantly enhances security by requiring users to provide two or more verification factors when attempting to access a system or network. These factors typically fall into three categories: something the user knows, something the user has, and something the user is. The integration of MFA into various systems, including network access control solutions, applications, and even device-level security, provides a more robust defense against unauthorized access and reduces the likelihood of successful cyberattacks, particularly those based on compromised credentials. However, while MFA is often seen as a security best practice, its advanced use cases provide even more layers of protection and offer unique solutions for specific challenges within the cybersecurity landscape.

One advanced use case for MFA involves integrating it with centralized authentication systems like TACACS. TACACS, which manages authentication, authorization, and accounting for network devices, plays a pivotal role in network security. By incorporating MFA into TACACS, organizations can enforce a multi-layered security approach for accessing critical network devices. This is particularly important in environments where network devices manage sensitive data or control critical systems, such as in financial institutions or healthcare networks. With TACACS enhanced by MFA, users attempting to access routers, switches, or firewalls must first authenticate with a standard username and password. Then, they are prompted to provide an additional factor of authentication, such as a one-time password (OTP) delivered via a mobile device or a biometric scan. This prevents attackers from gaining unauthorized access to these devices, even if they manage to steal or guess a valid user's password.

Another advanced use case for MFA can be seen in the implementation of adaptive authentication mechanisms. Adaptive authentication takes MFA a step further by dynamically adjusting the level of authentication required based on contextual factors. For instance, the system may require only basic password authentication when a user logs in from a trusted device within a secure network. However, if the same user tries to access the system from an unrecognized device, from a different geographical location, or during unusual hours, the system might prompt for additional authentication factors, such as a security question or a biometric scan. This flexible, context-aware approach to MFA reduces friction for users under normal conditions while providing heightened security when risky behavior or conditions are detected. Adaptive authentication systems, which combine machine learning and behavioral analytics, can learn from user patterns over time, improving their ability to detect anomalous activity and adjusting the authentication requirements accordingly.

MFA is also increasingly being used in the context of privileged access management (PAM). Privileged accounts, such as those used by system administrators or network engineers, have elevated access rights that allow them to make significant changes to systems, devices, and applications. Because these accounts provide powerful capabilities, they are often targeted by attackers. MFA significantly enhances the security of privileged accounts by requiring an additional layer of verification when accessing sensitive systems. For example, in a PAM environment, when a privileged user attempts to access a critical server or network device, they would first enter their username and password. Then, the system would require them to complete an MFA challenge, such as entering a code sent to a secure device or performing a biometric scan. This approach minimizes the risk of privileged account compromise, which is one of the most significant threats to network security. Additionally, PAM solutions integrated with MFA ensure that even if an attacker manages to steal login credentials, they will still face a second, substantial barrier before gaining access to critical systems.

Another advanced use case involves the use of MFA in cloud computing environments. As organizations increasingly migrate to the cloud, securing access to cloud-based applications and services becomes crucial. MFA offers a powerful solution for mitigating the risks associated with cloud adoption, where traditional perimeter defenses might not be as effective. In a cloud environment, MFA can be used to secure access to individual applications, entire cloud platforms, or even virtual machines running in a cloud data center. For example, users attempting to access a cloud-based storage solution or a virtual desktop infrastructure (VDI) environment can be required to provide multiple authentication factors, ensuring that only authorized individuals can access these cloud resources. Given the decentralized nature of cloud infrastructure, MFA provides an essential security layer that helps prevent unauthorized access and protects sensitive data stored in the cloud. Organizations that integrate MFA into their cloud security frameworks significantly reduce the risk of data breaches and ensure compliance with regulatory requirements such as GDPR, HIPAA, and PCI-DSS.

MFA also plays a crucial role in securing mobile access. As employees increasingly use mobile devices for work-related activities, securing these devices has become a top priority for many organizations. Mobile devices are often targeted by cybercriminals because they are portable, often connected to untrusted networks, and typically lack the robust security measures found in traditional desktop environments. MFA addresses these vulnerabilities by requiring additional authentication factors when users access corporate systems or applications from their mobile devices. For instance, a user may enter their standard password, and then the system may prompt them to provide a second factor of authentication, such as a fingerprint scan or an OTP delivered via a mobile authentication app. By securing mobile access with MFA, organizations can mitigate the risks associated with lost or stolen devices and ensure that only legitimate users can access sensitive corporate resources while on the go.

Another notable advanced use case for MFA is in securing the Internet of Things (IoT) devices. With the proliferation of IoT devices in both consumer and enterprise environments, ensuring that these devices are adequately secured has become increasingly important. Many IoT devices, such as smart cameras, industrial sensors, and connected machinery, are vulnerable to cyberattacks because they often rely on weak or default credentials for authentication. By implementing MFA for IoT devices, organizations can add an extra layer of security, requiring a secondary authentication factor to access these devices. For example, before a user can configure or manage a smart device, they may need to authenticate using both a password and a biometric factor, such as a facial scan. This advanced use case of MFA ensures that IoT devices, which are often considered weak points in cybersecurity, are protected against unauthorized access and manipulation.

Furthermore, MFA is being applied to secure remote access solutions, such as Virtual Private Networks (VPNs). VPNs are commonly used to provide employees with secure access to a company's internal network from remote locations. However, because VPNs provide access to critical internal resources, they are often targeted by attackers seeking to exploit weak authentication mechanisms. By integrating MFA into VPN solutions, organizations can add an extra layer of protection to this critical access point. For example, when an employee logs into a VPN, they may be required to provide their password and a one-time code sent via SMS or generated by an app. This MFA implementation ensures that even if an attacker manages to compromise a user's password, they will still need the second factor to gain access to the corporate network, reducing the risk of unauthorized access significantly.

The use of MFA in these advanced scenarios demonstrates how this security technology has evolved beyond basic authentication and become a powerful tool for securing access to a wide range of digital assets. As threats become more sophisticated and the attack surface expands, MFA serves as a crucial line of defense, ensuring that users are properly verified before being granted access to sensitive systems and data. By incorporating MFA into a variety of use cases, organizations can enhance their overall security posture, reduce the likelihood of successful attacks, and safeguard valuable resources across their network and systems.

Integrating TACACS with Identity Management Systems

In today's highly digitized and interconnected business environment, the security and management of user identities are paramount. Identity management systems (IMS) play a critical role in ensuring that only authorized individuals have access to sensitive information and network resources. At the same time, network devices, such as routers, switches, and firewalls, require robust access control mechanisms to protect them from unauthorized access and configuration changes. One of the most effective ways to manage authentication, authorization, and accounting (AAA) for network devices is through the use of the Terminal Access Controller Access-Control System (TACACS). Integrating TACACS with an identity management system creates a seamless and efficient security framework that allows organizations to centrally manage user identities and control access to network devices based on predefined policies. This integration not only strengthens security but also simplifies administrative workflows and enhances user experience.

The integration of TACACS with identity management systems enables organizations to centralize and streamline the process of user authentication and authorization. Identity management systems provide a comprehensive view of user identities, roles, and permissions across the organization. These systems allow administrators to define user access policies, assign roles, and manage the lifecycle of user accounts. When integrated with TACACS, the identity management system can feed user identity data into the TACACS protocol, allowing network administrators to apply these policies directly to network devices. This centralized approach ensures that all network devices are configured consistently and that access controls are enforced according to the user's role and responsibilities within the organization. For example, network administrators can define a policy that grants read-only access to certain users for monitoring purposes while restricting others to full administrative rights for configuration and maintenance tasks.

Furthermore, integrating TACACS with identity management systems allows for more granular control over user access. Identity management systems typically support role-based access control (RBAC), which enables administrators to assign specific roles to users based on their job functions. These roles can then be mapped to the corresponding permissions within TACACS, ensuring that each user has the appropriate level of access to network devices. For instance, a network engineer may require full access to configure network devices, while a junior technician may only need limited access to view device configurations. By integrating TACACS with the identity management system, administrators can automatically enforce these access policies based on the user's assigned role, eliminating the need for manual configuration of access controls on individual network devices. This not only saves time but also reduces the risk of misconfigurations or human error.

In addition to simplifying the management of user access, the integration of TACACS with identity management systems enhances security by enforcing consistent access controls across the entire network. As organizations grow and expand, the number of network devices and users increases, making it challenging to manage access manually. TACACS allows for the centralized management of access controls for network devices, while identity management systems ensure that user identities are accurately maintained and kept up to date. When a user's role or permissions change within the identity management system, those changes are automatically reflected in the TACACS policies, ensuring that the user's access rights are updated across all network devices. This level of automation helps to ensure that users are only granted access to the resources they need and that access is promptly revoked when no longer necessary.

One of the key benefits of integrating TACACS with identity management systems is the ability to provide a more seamless user experience. In many organizations, users need to authenticate themselves multiple times to access different systems and network resources. This can lead to a fragmented and cumbersome experience, where users must remember multiple credentials and undergo redundant authentication processes. By integrating TACACS with an identity management system, users can leverage single sign-on (SSO) capabilities, enabling them to authenticate once and gain access to both network devices and other resources across the organization. With SSO, users are not required to repeatedly enter their credentials, reducing friction and improving productivity. Additionally, this integration ensures that user identities are managed consistently across different systems, making it easier for administrators to maintain accurate records and track user activity.

Moreover, integrating TACACS with identity management systems enhances the audit and compliance capabilities of an organization. Regulatory frameworks such as HIPAA, PCI-DSS, and SOX often require organizations to maintain detailed records of who accessed network devices and what actions were performed. By leveraging the centralized logging capabilities of TACACS and the identity management system, administrators can generate comprehensive audit trails that track user activity across the entire network. This integration ensures that all access attempts, including successful logins and failed login attempts, are logged and can be reviewed for compliance purposes. These audit trails also help to identify potential security threats, such as unauthorized access attempts or suspicious behavior, enabling administrators to take appropriate action before a breach occurs. In environments where sensitive data is stored or processed, the ability to generate detailed and reliable audit logs is critical for meeting regulatory requirements and demonstrating adherence to security standards.

The integration of TACACS with identity management systems also supports the use of multi-factor authentication (MFA) to further enhance security. MFA requires users to provide two or more forms of authentication before gaining access to network devices or other resources. By integrating TACACS with an identity management system that supports MFA, administrators can enforce this additional layer of security for network device access. For example, users may be required to enter their username and password, followed by a one-time passcode sent to their mobile device or a biometric scan. This multi-layered approach significantly reduces the risk of unauthorized access, even if a user's password is compromised. By incorporating MFA into the authentication process, organizations can strengthen their defenses against cyber threats and ensure that only authorized users can access critical network devices.

Another significant advantage of integrating TACACS with identity management systems is the ability to manage the lifecycle of user accounts more effectively. As employees join, move within, or leave an organization, their access rights must be updated to reflect their current roles. Manual management of user accounts can be time-consuming and error-prone, especially in large organizations with many users and devices. By integrating TACACS with an identity management system, administrators can automate the process of updating user accounts and access permissions, ensuring that users are granted access to the appropriate resources based on their current role and responsibilities. For instance, when an employee transitions to a new department, the identity management system can automatically update their access rights, and these changes will be reflected in the TACACS policy. Similarly, when an employee leaves the organization, their access to network devices can be promptly revoked, preventing potential security risks associated with orphaned accounts.

The integration of TACACS with identity management systems also facilitates better scalability as organizations expand. As the number of users and network devices increases, the ability to centrally manage access policies becomes even more important. By integrating TACACS with an identity management system, organizations can scale their network access controls without the need for manual configuration of each device. New users can be automatically assigned the appropriate access rights based on their role, and these rights can be enforced across all network devices through TACACS. This scalable approach helps organizations maintain security and consistency as their network infrastructure grows and evolves.

Incorporating TACACS with identity management systems not only simplifies the management of user access but also enhances the overall security posture of the organization. The ability to centrally manage user identities, roles, and permissions ensures that access controls are applied consistently across all network devices, reducing the risk of unauthorized access and misconfigurations. Additionally, the integration streamlines administrative workflows, improves the user experience, and strengthens compliance efforts by providing comprehensive audit logs and enabling the enforcement of multi-factor authentication. This integration is a powerful tool for organizations looking to safeguard their network resources, improve operational efficiency, and stay ahead of evolving cybersecurity threats.

Performance Tuning and Optimization

Performance tuning and optimization are critical aspects of network and system administration that ensure the efficiency, reliability, and scalability of IT infrastructures. Whether it is network devices, databases, or application servers, optimizing performance involves a combination of configuring settings, monitoring performance, and making necessary adjustments to meet the demands of growing environments. For many organizations, the goal of performance tuning is to maximize throughput, minimize latency, and ensure that all systems operate smoothly under peak loads. These objectives are not static and require continuous adjustments as networks evolve and business requirements change. The process of performance optimization is multifaceted, often involving hardware upgrades, software configuration adjustments, and improvements in the underlying architecture. Effective performance tuning is essential not only for providing high-quality service but also for reducing operational costs and ensuring that systems can handle unexpected surges in traffic or workload.

At the core of performance tuning is the need for proper monitoring. Without detailed insights into the system's performance, it is difficult to identify bottlenecks or inefficiencies. One of the primary tools used for performance monitoring is network management software, which tracks the traffic flow across network devices. This data can reveal patterns such as high bandwidth usage, packet loss, or long latency, which may indicate areas of the network that need optimization.

Similarly, monitoring the CPU and memory usage of servers can help administrators identify resource constraints that could lead to slower performance or downtime. By collecting performance data continuously, administrators can spot trends over time and predict potential issues before they become critical. Monitoring tools can also be used to track response times and failure rates, allowing for quick troubleshooting in the event of performance degradation.

Once performance data has been collected, the next step in the optimization process is identifying bottlenecks. Bottlenecks can occur at various points in a network or system, such as at the data link layer of a network, in the processing capacity of a server, or within the database query layer. Identifying these bottlenecks involves analyzing performance metrics such as throughput, latency, and packet loss to pinpoint where traffic or data is being delayed. For example, if a network device is experiencing high traffic loads, it may be necessary to increase bandwidth, upgrade hardware, or implement more efficient traffic management strategies, such as Quality of Service (QoS) controls, to prioritize important traffic over less critical data. Additionally, database optimization may involve tuning queries or indexing strategies to reduce response times and increase transaction throughput. Addressing these bottlenecks often requires a combination of hardware upgrades and software tuning to strike a balance between resources and demand.

Optimizing network and system performance also requires managing load distribution effectively. Load balancing plays a critical role in preventing any single server or network device from becoming overwhelmed by traffic. By distributing the load across multiple resources, organizations can prevent server overloads, reduce latency, and ensure higher availability. In large-scale environments, where traffic patterns can be unpredictable, load balancing solutions can automatically adjust to changes in demand, providing more capacity during peak periods and redistributing traffic when needed. Load balancing can be applied not only to network traffic but also to databases, application servers, and other components of the IT infrastructure. In cloud environments, load balancing is often automated, enabling dynamic scaling of resources based on real-time demand, which can significantly enhance performance and reduce costs.

In addition to load balancing, performance tuning and optimization also involve reducing resource contention. Resource contention occurs when multiple processes or users attempt to access the same resources at the same time, causing delays or slow performance. In network environments, this might involve managing the allocation of bandwidth to ensure that critical applications or users have access to the necessary resources without interference. Similarly, in multi-threaded applications, contention for CPU or memory resources can slow down performance, requiring administrators to implement strategies such as process prioritization or the use of caching mechanisms to reduce the workload on critical systems. Resource contention can also be managed by fine-tuning system settings and ensuring that processes are allocated appropriately to avoid overloading any particular resource.

Another key aspect of performance optimization is ensuring that systems and networks are configured for redundancy and fault tolerance. Redundancy ensures that there is always a backup available in case a primary system or network path fails. This is essential for maintaining high availability and performance, particularly in mission-critical environments where downtime is not an option. Redundancy can be achieved at various levels, from network equipment like routers and switches to power supplies and even entire data centers. Failover systems can automatically redirect traffic or workload to backup resources in the event of failure, ensuring that performance is not impacted. While redundancy introduces additional complexity into the network design, it is necessary to maintain high performance under all conditions and avoid system failures that could lead to prolonged outages or degraded service.

In parallel with redundancy, ensuring scalability is also a critical part of performance optimization. As networks grow and traffic increases, it is essential to scale resources to meet the demands of the expanding environment. Scalability can be achieved by adding more hardware resources, such as additional servers, storage devices, or network switches, or by optimizing the existing infrastructure. For instance, in cloud environments, performance tuning often involves dynamically allocating more compute power or storage as needed, a process that can be automated based on traffic patterns or workload fluctuations. Scaling horizontally by adding more machines or nodes to a network can distribute the load across more resources, whereas vertical scaling involves upgrading the capacity of existing hardware. Both strategies are important for ensuring that systems can handle increased traffic without compromising performance.

Database performance is another area that requires specific tuning for optimization. For applications that rely heavily on database interactions, slow database queries or inefficient indexing can lead to significant performance degradation. Optimizing database performance involves tuning queries, creating efficient indexes, and ensuring that the database schema is well-structured for the type of queries being executed. Additionally, implementing caching mechanisms at various levels, such as query caching or result caching, can significantly reduce the load on the database by storing frequently accessed data in faster storage locations, allowing for quicker retrieval. Ensuring that databases are properly indexed and optimized for the specific workload they are handling can improve response times and overall system performance.

Performance tuning also involves ensuring that the security measures in place do not interfere with the overall system performance. Security measures such as firewalls, encryption, and intrusion detection systems are essential for protecting networks from threats, but they can sometimes introduce latency or consume system resources. Optimizing security settings to strike a balance between protection and performance is critical. For example, firewalls and intrusion detection systems should be configured to prioritize critical traffic and reduce the overhead of monitoring low-risk activity. Similarly, encryption should be implemented efficiently to minimize the impact on data transfer speeds while maintaining a high level of security.

To achieve optimal performance, regular testing and benchmarking are also essential. By simulating traffic and workloads under different conditions, administrators can assess how the system behaves under stress and identify areas for improvement. This testing should be done regularly to ensure that performance remains consistent even as the environment evolves. Benchmarking tools can help quantify the impact of specific changes and provide valuable data to guide future optimization efforts.

Ultimately, performance tuning and optimization are ongoing processes that require constant attention and adjustment. As network traffic grows, new applications are introduced, and business requirements change, administrators must continuously monitor and adjust system performance to ensure that resources are used efficiently and that users experience optimal service levels. By applying a combination of monitoring, tuning, resource management, and scalability strategies, organizations can maintain high-performance systems and networks that meet the demands of their users and business objectives.

Regulatory Compliance with TACACS

Regulatory compliance has become a critical concern for organizations worldwide as governments and regulatory bodies continue to impose stringent data protection, privacy, and security standards. In industries such as healthcare, finance, and telecommunications, organizations are required to implement robust security measures to protect sensitive data and ensure the confidentiality, integrity, and availability of their systems. One of the ways to meet these compliance requirements is by using access control mechanisms that securely manage and monitor user activity. The Terminal Access Controller Access-Control System (TACACS) is an authentication, authorization, and accounting (AAA) protocol commonly used for managing access to network devices. TACACS helps organizations maintain security by controlling who can access network devices, what actions they can perform, and keeping detailed logs of all activity. Integrating TACACS with regulatory compliance requirements ensures that organizations meet necessary legal and industry standards, especially in environments where data security and access control are paramount.

Compliance frameworks such as the General Data Protection Regulation (GDPR), Health Insurance Portability and Accountability Act (HIPAA), and Payment Card Industry Data Security Standard (PCI-DSS) impose strict regulations on how organizations handle sensitive data. In many cases, these frameworks require organizations to implement strict access control measures to prevent unauthorized access to systems and data. TACACS can play a vital role in meeting these requirements by offering granular control over who can access network devices and ensuring that all access attempts are logged and monitored. For example, HIPAA mandates that healthcare organizations implement role-based access controls (RBAC) to restrict access to electronic health records (EHRs) and other sensitive medical data. TACACS supports RBAC, allowing administrators to assign specific permissions to users based on their role within the organization, ensuring that only authorized personnel can access certain systems and data. By integrating TACACS into the organization's security infrastructure, administrators can ensure that access control policies are consistently enforced across all network devices.

Furthermore, regulatory compliance often requires detailed logging of all user activity, especially when accessing critical systems or sensitive data. Both GDPR and PCI-DSS, for example, require organizations to maintain comprehensive audit logs to track user actions and ensure accountability. TACACS supports accounting, which means it generates detailed logs of all user interactions with network devices, including login attempts, executed commands, and configuration changes. These logs are invaluable for demonstrating compliance with regulatory requirements, as they provide a clear audit trail that can be reviewed during internal or external audits. In industries where data protection is essential, the ability to track and document user actions in real-time is critical for identifying potential security breaches and ensuring that organizations meet regulatory standards. The logs produced by TACACS can be securely stored and reviewed by security teams to detect suspicious activity, identify potential violations, and take corrective action when necessary.

In addition to logging, TACACS enables organizations to enforce the principle of least privilege, which is a key tenet of many regulatory frameworks. The principle of least privilege ensures that users have access only to the resources they need to perform their job functions and nothing more. This is crucial for maintaining security and reducing the risk of data breaches or misuse. TACACS allows administrators to define detailed access control policies based on the user's role, ensuring that users only have access to the specific devices and resources required for their tasks. For instance, a network administrator may need full access to configure devices, while a network technician may only need read-only access to monitor the system's status. By restricting access based on the user's role and responsibilities, organizations can better comply with regulations that require strict access control and minimize the risk of insider threats.

Another important compliance requirement that TACACS helps organizations meet is the need for multi-factor authentication (MFA). Regulatory frameworks like PCI-DSS and NIST SP 800-53 require organizations to implement MFA as an additional layer of protection for sensitive systems and data. TACACS can be integrated with MFA solutions, allowing organizations to require users to authenticate using multiple factors before gaining access to critical network devices. For example, users may be required to provide both a password and a one-time passcode sent to their mobile device or generated by an authentication app. MFA significantly reduces the risk of unauthorized access by adding an additional layer of security beyond traditional password-based authentication. By integrating TACACS with MFA, organizations can ensure that they meet regulatory requirements for strong authentication and further enhance the security of their network devices.

Regulatory compliance also mandates that organizations implement regular reviews of user access rights and promptly revoke access when it is no longer required. This is particularly important when employees change roles, leave the organization, or are terminated. TACACS allows administrators to automate access revocation based on changes in user status, ensuring that users who no longer require access are promptly removed from the system. For example, if an employee leaves the company or is reassigned to a different department, their access to network devices should be revoked to prevent unauthorized access. Regular reviews of user access rights are also necessary to ensure that access controls remain aligned with the organization's evolving needs. With TACACS, administrators can easily track changes to user permissions and ensure that users only have access to the systems and resources they are authorized to use. This helps maintain compliance with regulations that require periodic access reviews and prompt removal of unnecessary privileges.

Another significant aspect of regulatory compliance is ensuring that sensitive data is protected during transmission. TACACS supports secure communication protocols, such as Secure Sockets Layer (SSL) and Transport Layer Security (TLS), to encrypt data between the client and server. This encryption ensures that sensitive information, such as user credentials and configuration changes, is protected during transmission across the network. In many regulatory frameworks, including GDPR and HIPAA, encryption is a critical requirement for protecting sensitive data. By ensuring that TACACS traffic is encrypted, organizations can prevent unauthorized interception and ensure that user authentication and other sensitive information remain secure. This encryption capability is vital in environments where data privacy and security are regulated, helping organizations meet the stringent requirements for protecting sensitive information.

In industries with high compliance requirements, such as finance and healthcare, organizations must also implement measures to protect against insider threats. Insider threats can come from employees, contractors, or other trusted individuals who have access to critical systems and data. TACACS helps mitigate this risk by providing detailed auditing and logging capabilities that allow organizations to track and monitor user actions on network devices. By maintaining detailed logs of who accessed a system, what changes were made, and when they occurred, TACACS enables organizations to detect suspicious activity and respond to potential insider threats before they escalate. The ability to monitor and audit user activity is crucial for maintaining compliance with regulatory frameworks that require organizations to implement controls to detect and prevent insider threats.

Integrating TACACS into an organization's security infrastructure provides a robust solution for meeting regulatory compliance requirements. By offering centralized access control, granular permission settings, detailed auditing, support for multi-factor authentication, and secure communication, TACACS helps organizations adhere to strict data protection and security standards. Compliance with frameworks such as GDPR, HIPAA, and PCI-DSS is not only necessary for avoiding penalties and legal consequences but also for safeguarding sensitive information and ensuring that the organization's systems are secure from potential threats. The ability to use TACACS to enforce compliance requirements across network devices ensures that organizations can maintain the confidentiality, integrity, and availability of their systems while meeting the ever-evolving demands of regulatory frameworks.

Case Study: TACACS in Service Provider Networks

In the context of service provider networks, where large-scale infrastructure is in place to deliver a variety of services to end-users, managing and securing access to network devices is a critical task. One of the most effective ways to ensure that only authorized personnel can access critical network devices and perform necessary configurations is through the use of TACACS (Terminal Access Controller Access-Control System). Service providers, whether they offer internet, telecommunications, or cloud services, face significant challenges in maintaining network security, especially when it comes to controlling and monitoring access to routers, switches, firewalls, and other network components. Integrating TACACS into their network infrastructure offers a robust and centralized solution to these challenges, helping ensure compliance with security policies and providing enhanced control over who can access specific network devices.

A leading global telecommunications service provider faced the challenge of securing their vast network of routers, switches, and firewalls spread across multiple regions and data centers. With thousands of network devices to manage, controlling and auditing access to these devices had become a cumbersome and error-prone process. Network administrators had to rely on individual access control configurations on each device, which not only consumed valuable time but also created potential security gaps. The company needed a scalable and efficient way to centralize authentication, authorization, and accounting (AAA) for network devices while maintaining granular control over user permissions. TACACS emerged as the ideal solution to address these challenges.

By integrating TACACS into their network infrastructure, the telecommunications provider was able to centralize the authentication process, eliminating the need for managing access on individual devices. TACACS enabled the provider to create a centralized authentication server that could manage all user access attempts across their entire network. This integration streamlined the process of adding new users, updating user permissions, and ensuring that each user had the appropriate access levels to perform their duties. The service provider implemented a role-based access control (RBAC) model, where network administrators, engineers, and support staff were granted different levels of access based on their roles within the organization. For example, a senior network engineer had full administrative access to configure routers and switches, while a junior technician was granted read-only access to monitor network health and troubleshoot issues. This level of control ensured that users were only able to access the systems and resources required for their job, following the principle of least privilege.

One of the key benefits of implementing TACACS in this service provider network was the ability to enforce multi-factor authentication (MFA) for sensitive network devices. As part of the service provider's security strategy, MFA was introduced to further strengthen access control for privileged accounts. With TACACS, administrators could configure MFA for users attempting to access critical network devices, requiring them to provide not only their username and password but also a second form of authentication, such as a one-time passcode sent to their mobile device. This added layer of security helped mitigate the risk of unauthorized access, especially in scenarios where credentials could be compromised. By integrating TACACS with an MFA solution, the provider significantly reduced the chances of attackers gaining access to sensitive network devices, even if they had obtained valid credentials through phishing or other means.

Another advantage of using TACACS in the service provider network was its ability to generate detailed accounting logs that recorded every user action on network devices. This logging capability was essential for compliance with industry regulations and internal security policies. The service provider needed to maintain an audit trail of who accessed which devices, when they accessed them, and what actions they performed. This was especially important in regulated industries, such as telecommunications, where data security and accountability are paramount. With TACACS, administrators were able to automatically capture and store detailed logs of user activity, including configuration changes, troubleshooting tasks, and administrative actions. These logs were securely stored and could be accessed later for review or forensic analysis in the event of a security incident. By having this detailed logging in place, the service provider ensured compliance with regulatory standards such as the General Data Protection Regulation (GDPR) and the Payment Card Industry Data Security Standard (PCI-DSS).

The integration of TACACS also provided the service provider with enhanced scalability as their network grew. Service providers are constantly expanding their infrastructure to meet increasing demand and provide services to more customers. As new network devices were added to the infrastructure, the provider was able to automatically integrate these devices into the TACACS-based authentication system, ensuring consistent access control across the entire network. This scalability was crucial for the provider, as it allowed them to quickly and efficiently scale their network without sacrificing security or access control. Furthermore, the centralized nature of TACACS made it easier to manage user access as the provider's network expanded into new regions and data centers. Instead of manually configuring access on each new device, administrators could rely on the TACACS server to handle all authentication requests, simplifying the onboarding process for new devices.

One of the more complex challenges the service provider faced was ensuring that access control remained consistent across geographically distributed networks. With multiple data centers located in different regions, network administrators needed a solution that could centralize access management without compromising performance. TACACS provided a solution by allowing administrators to configure multiple TACACS servers in a distributed manner. These servers could be strategically placed in different regions to ensure that authentication requests were processed locally, reducing latency and improving performance. Additionally, TACACS allowed for redundancy, ensuring that if one server failed, another could take over without disrupting access control across the network. This distributed setup ensured that the service provider's network remained secure and accessible, even in the event of hardware or network failures.

Furthermore, the service provider integrated TACACS with their existing network monitoring and security information and event management (SIEM) systems to enhance real-time security monitoring and incident response capabilities. The logs generated by TACACS, which contained detailed information about user access and actions on network devices, were fed into the SIEM system for real-time analysis. This integration allowed security teams to correlate TACACS logs with other network activity data, such as traffic patterns and alerts from firewalls or intrusion detection systems. By correlating data from multiple sources, the provider could detect potential security incidents more quickly and respond proactively to mitigate risks. For example, if an unauthorized user attempted to access a network device, the SIEM system could generate an alert, prompting security teams to investigate and take appropriate action.

The integration of TACACS in the service provider network ultimately improved security, streamlined administrative workflows, and enhanced scalability. By centralizing access control, enforcing MFA, generating detailed logs, and ensuring compliance with industry regulations, the provider was able to manage a vast and complex network with greater efficiency and security. The ability to scale seamlessly as the network expanded allowed the provider to meet the growing demand for their services while maintaining a high level of security. This case study demonstrates how TACACS can play a critical role in securing and managing access to network devices in large-scale service provider environments, providing both operational benefits and enhanced security.

Merging Trends in Network Access Control

Network access control (NAC) has evolved significantly in recent years as organizations increasingly face new challenges in securing their IT environments. As cyber threats become more sophisticated and businesses rely more heavily on digital platforms, the need for robust and adaptive access control mechanisms has never been greater. Merging trends in network access control reflect a shift toward more comprehensive, flexible, and dynamic security frameworks that go beyond traditional methods of controlling access to network resources.

These emerging trends are driven by the growing complexity of networks, the rise of cloud computing, the proliferation of mobile devices, and the increasing adoption of zero trust security models. As a result, organizations are leveraging innovative technologies and approaches to ensure that only authorized users and devices can access critical systems and data.

One of the most significant trends in network access control is the adoption of the zero trust security model. Zero trust operates on the principle that no user or device, regardless of whether it is inside or outside the organization's network, should be implicitly trusted. This model assumes that every access attempt is a potential threat, and therefore, all users and devices must be continuously authenticated, authorized, and validated before being granted access to any resource. Zero trust security goes beyond traditional perimeter-based security models, which focus on protecting the network boundary. Instead, it emphasizes securing access at every point in the network, whether the user is accessing resources from the corporate network, a remote location, or the cloud. Zero trust security models require organizations to implement stringent access controls, multi-factor authentication (MFA), and detailed monitoring to ensure that only legitimate users can access sensitive data.

Another important trend in network access control is the integration of identity and access management (IAM) solutions with NAC systems. IAM platforms are designed to manage user identities, enforce access policies, and ensure that only authorized individuals can access specific resources. By integrating IAM with NAC, organizations can create a unified framework that not only manages authentication and authorization but also ensures that access controls are consistently enforced across the entire network. This integration enables organizations to implement role-based access control (RBAC), where users are assigned specific permissions based on their job roles or responsibilities. This ensures that employees, contractors, and partners only have access to the resources they need to perform their tasks, reducing the risk of unauthorized access to sensitive information. Furthermore, the combination of IAM and NAC enables organizations to enforce policies that ensure compliance with regulatory requirements such as the General Data Protection Regulation (GDPR) or the Health Insurance Portability and Accountability Act (HIPAA).

The increased reliance on cloud computing and hybrid IT environments is also shaping the future of network access control. As more businesses migrate their applications and services to the cloud, they face new challenges in ensuring secure access to cloud resources. Cloud-based applications often require different access control mechanisms than traditional on-premises systems, making it essential for organizations to adapt their NAC strategies to accommodate this shift. Cloud access security brokers (CASBs) are increasingly being used to bridge the gap between on-premises and cloud-based resources. CASBs provide visibility into cloud usage and enforce security policies for cloud applications, ensuring that access controls are applied consistently across all environments. This trend is also driving the adoption of single sign-on (SSO) and multi-factor authentication (MFA) solutions to simplify the user experience while maintaining strong security controls for accessing cloud services.

Mobile devices are another factor influencing the evolution of network access control. As the use of smartphones, tablets, and laptops continues to increase, managing access to network resources from these devices presents unique challenges. Employees often use personal mobile devices to access corporate applications, leading to concerns about data security and privacy. In response to this, many organizations are adopting mobile device management (MDM) solutions, which allow them to monitor, secure, and control mobile devices that access corporate networks. MDM solutions enable organizations to enforce security policies such as encryption, remote wipe, and secure access to corporate resources, ensuring that mobile devices do not become a weak point in the network security infrastructure. Furthermore, integrating MDM with NAC allows organizations to enforce access controls based on the security posture of mobile devices. For example, a device that is not encrypted or does not have the latest security updates may be denied access to critical resources, reducing the risk of data breaches.

The rise of artificial intelligence (AI) and machine learning (ML) is also influencing the future of network access control. AI and ML technologies are being used to enhance access control mechanisms by enabling systems to automatically detect and respond to potential security threats. For example, machine learning algorithms can analyze user behavior and network traffic patterns to identify anomalies that may indicate unauthorized access or malicious activity. By continuously learning from past data, these systems can become more accurate over time, improving the ability to detect emerging threats and reduce false positives. AI-driven NAC solutions can also automate the process of granting or revoking access based on real-time risk assessments, making access control more dynamic and responsive to changes in the network environment. This allows organizations to implement adaptive access control policies that adjust the level of authentication or authorization required based on the context of the access request, such as the user's location, device, or the sensitivity of the requested resource.

As organizations continue to adopt more flexible and dynamic security models, the need for integrated network access control systems becomes increasingly important. Traditional methods of managing access based solely on user credentials or IP addresses are no longer sufficient to address the complex security challenges posed by modern IT environments. Emerging NAC solutions that integrate with a variety of security technologies, including IAM, MFA, CASB, MDM, and AI-driven analytics, offer a more holistic approach to securing access to network resources. These solutions enable organizations to implement granular access policies that are tailored to the specific needs of their users, devices, and applications, ensuring that access is always appropriately controlled based on the level of trust associated with each access attempt.

Additionally, as organizations adopt more decentralized and distributed network architectures, such as edge computing and the Internet of Things (IoT), NAC systems will need to be able to manage access to a wide range of devices and endpoints. IoT devices, in particular, present a significant challenge for traditional NAC solutions, as they often lack the same security features and management capabilities as traditional computing devices. In response, next-generation NAC systems are being designed to support IoT security by enabling organizations to define access policies for IoT devices and ensure that they are securely integrated into the network. This will be essential as the number of connected devices continues to grow, and as organizations look to ensure that their network access control systems can scale to meet the demands of a rapidly changing digital landscape.

As the landscape of network access control continues to evolve, organizations will need to adopt more comprehensive and adaptive security strategies. The trends driving the future of NAC reflect a shift toward more integrated, automated, and context-aware solutions that can meet the complex demands of modern IT environments. By embracing these emerging trends, organizations can enhance their security posture, streamline access management processes, and better protect their critical assets from a wide range of security threats. As the use of cloud services, mobile devices, AI, and IoT devices continues to expand, NAC will play a crucial role in ensuring that organizations can manage and secure access to their networks and resources, regardless of where or how those resources are accessed.

TACACS and IoT Security

The Internet of Things (IoT) has become a major driver of digital transformation across industries, enabling organizations to collect valuable data, optimize operations, and offer new services. From smart appliances to industrial sensors, IoT devices are becoming increasingly ubiquitous. However, as the number of connected devices grows, so do the risks associated with their security. Unlike traditional IT systems, IoT devices often have limited processing power, memory, and security features, which makes them vulnerable to cyberattacks. Securing IoT devices and the networks they connect to is an essential priority for organizations seeking to protect their data and infrastructure. One of the most effective ways to manage and secure access to IoT devices is through the integration of TACACS (Terminal Access Controller Access-Control System). TACACS, a widely used protocol for managing authentication, authorization, and accounting (AAA), offers a comprehensive solution for controlling access to network devices and can be extended to IoT environments to enhance security.

IoT devices often operate in complex, distributed environments, making it difficult to secure them with traditional security mechanisms. Unlike conventional computers or servers, IoT devices often lack robust built-in security features, such as firewalls, encryption, and access controls. This makes them prime targets for cybercriminals who seek to exploit vulnerabilities to gain unauthorized

138

access or launch attacks on the network. To address these security gaps, organizations must implement a multi-layered security approach that includes robust authentication mechanisms, secure communication channels, and real-time monitoring. By integrating TACACS into IoT security frameworks, organizations can centralize authentication and authorization processes for IoT devices and ensure that only authorized users and devices can access critical resources.

The first key advantage of integrating TACACS into IoT security is the ability to provide centralized control over access. In IoT environments, especially those involving large numbers of devices, it is essential to have a system that can manage user access efficiently and consistently. TACACS allows administrators to define who can access IoT devices, what actions they can perform, and under what conditions. By using TACACS, organizations can enforce role-based access control (RBAC), ensuring that different users and devices have appropriate permissions based on their roles and responsibilities. For example, a network engineer might be granted full access to configure IoT sensors in a smart factory, while a regular employee may only have read-only access to monitor data from those sensors. This granular control ensures that IoT devices are not exposed to unnecessary risk by granting excessive permissions to users or devices that do not require them.

Another significant benefit of TACACS in securing IoT devices is its support for multi-factor authentication (MFA). MFA is increasingly recognized as a critical security measure to mitigate the risks associated with compromised credentials. In IoT environments, where devices are often distributed across various locations and networks, ensuring that only authorized users can access IoT devices is vital. TACACS can be integrated with MFA solutions to provide an additional layer of security. When a user attempts to access an IoT device, TACACS can require them to authenticate using two or more factors, such as a password and a one-time passcode sent to their mobile device, or a biometric scan. This significantly reduces the chances of unauthorized access, even if a user's credentials are compromised, and helps ensure that only trusted individuals can manage or configure sensitive IoT devices.

Moreover, the integration of TACACS with IoT security enhances accountability and auditing capabilities. One of the challenges in managing IoT devices is maintaining an audit trail of who accessed which device, when they accessed it, and what actions they performed. This is especially important in industries where compliance with regulatory standards, such as healthcare or finance, is a concern. TACACS provides detailed accounting and logging capabilities, allowing administrators to capture and store logs of all access attempts to IoT devices. These logs include critical information, such as the identity of the user or device requesting access, the time and date of the access attempt, and any actions taken during the session. By integrating TACACS into IoT security, organizations can easily generate reports and review logs to ensure compliance with industry regulations and detect any suspicious activity. This level of visibility is essential for identifying potential security breaches, auditing user behavior, and meeting the requirements of data protection regulations.

One of the major security challenges in IoT environments is the diversity of devices and the lack of standardization. IoT devices can vary widely in terms of their capabilities, protocols, and security features. Some devices may support advanced security features, while others may have minimal security controls. As a result, securing access to these devices requires a flexible and adaptable approach. TACACS offers a versatile solution that can be customized to work with a wide range of IoT devices, regardless of their security capabilities. By centralizing access management through TACACS, organizations can apply consistent authentication, authorization, and accounting policies across all IoT devices, ensuring that even devices with limited security features are subject to the same access controls. This flexibility allows organizations to secure their entire IoT ecosystem, regardless of the device type or its inherent security features.

In addition to managing access to IoT devices, TACACS can also be used to enforce security policies related to device configuration and management. In many IoT environments, devices are often configured and maintained remotely, which introduces additional risks if not properly managed. TACACS allows administrators to enforce strict policies around device configuration, ensuring that only authorized users can make changes to the settings of IoT devices. For example, administrators can configure TACACS to allow only authorized personnel to update the firmware of IoT sensors or change their network settings. This ensures that any changes made to the devices are legitimate and do not introduce vulnerabilities that could be exploited by attackers. Furthermore, by logging all configuration changes, TACACS provides an audit trail that helps organizations track and review any modifications made to their IoT devices, enhancing overall security.

The integration of TACACS with IoT security also facilitates the enforcement of the principle of least privilege. In IoT environments, where devices can have varying levels of sensitivity and importance, it is crucial to limit access based on the principle of least privilege, which ensures that users and devices only have the minimum level of access necessary to perform their tasks. TACACS allows organizations to create detailed access control policies that restrict access to IoT devices based on the user's role, the device's sensitivity, and the specific task being performed. For instance, an administrator might need full access to configure a critical IoT device, while a support technician may only need access to monitor its status. By enforcing this principle, TACACS helps reduce the risk of unauthorized access or accidental misconfigurations that could compromise the security of the IoT environment.

As the number of IoT devices continues to grow, securing them becomes an increasingly complex and urgent priority. Integrating TACACS into IoT security provides organizations with a powerful tool to manage access, enforce policies, and enhance visibility into device activity. By centralizing authentication, enabling multi-factor authentication, and providing detailed logging and auditing capabilities, TACACS helps organizations protect their IoT environments from unauthorized access and potential security threats. The flexibility and scalability of TACACS make it an ideal solution for securing a wide range of IoT devices, from industrial sensors to smart home appliances, and ensuring that access controls are consistently applied across the network. This level of security is essential as IoT devices become more embedded in our daily lives and business operations, making it possible for organizations to harness the full potential of IoT while minimizing the risks associated with its use.

Implementing TACACS+ in Industrial Control Systems (ICS)

The integration of Terminal Access Controller Access-Control System Plus (TACACS+) within Industrial Control Systems (ICS) represents a pivotal step in enhancing the security, accountability, and operational efficiency of critical infrastructure environments. TACACS+ is a centralized authentication, authorization, and accounting (AAA) protocol, which has long been employed in traditional IT environments to regulate access to network devices and systems. Its application within ICS environments, however, brings unique challenges and considerations due to the specific characteristics and constraints of these operational technologies.

Industrial Control Systems often govern essential processes within sectors such as energy, manufacturing, water treatment, transportation, and chemical processing. Unlike traditional IT systems, ICS prioritize availability and deterministic behavior over other objectives like confidentiality or data integrity. This focus on uninterrupted operations creates a delicate balance when introducing security protocols like TACACS+, which inherently add layers of control and potential latency. ICS environments typically contain legacy devices and proprietary protocols not initially designed with modern security architectures in mind. Therefore, implementing TACACS+ within ICS demands a comprehensive approach that considers both technical integration and operational impact.

The primary advantage of implementing TACACS+ in ICS is the ability to centralize and enforce user access policies across multiple devices and platforms. By deploying a TACACS+ server, administrators can ensure that only authenticated and authorized personnel are able to execute specific commands on devices such as programmable logic controllers (PLCs), remote terminal units (RTUs), human-machine interfaces (HMIs), and other critical control elements. This level of control mitigates the risk of unauthorized access and malicious activities, including accidental misconfigurations that could lead to costly downtime or safety incidents. Furthermore, TACACS+ offers granular command authorization, which allows administrators to define precise permissions for each user or group, limiting their ability to execute sensitive or potentially harmful operations.

Another key feature of TACACS+ is its robust accounting capability. In an ICS setting, detailed logging of user actions is vital not only for forensic investigations in the event of an incident but also for meeting regulatory compliance requirements. Logs generated by TACACS+ servers can provide comprehensive records of every command issued, every login attempt, and every configuration change performed on network-connected ICS devices. These logs serve as invaluable resources for security teams, auditors, and operations personnel who need to maintain visibility and control over the system's security posture. The ability to correlate TACACS+ logs with other security information and event management (SIEM) data streams further enhances the detection and response capabilities of industrial cybersecurity operations.

Despite these benefits, there are critical challenges associated with deploying TACACS+ within ICS. One major consideration is the need to maintain system availability and avoid introducing additional points of failure. TACACS+ servers themselves must be resilient, employing high-availability configurations and fault-tolerant designs to prevent disruptions in access control. Any unavailability of the TACACS+ server could result in operational personnel being locked out of essential devices, leading to potential production halts or safety risks. To address this, many ICS environments implement fallback authentication methods, such as local user accounts with predefined emergency credentials, to ensure continuity of operations during TACACS+ outages.

Latency and network reliability are additional concerns. Industrial environments may operate in geographically dispersed or harsh conditions where network connectivity is intermittent or constrained by legacy infrastructure. The overhead introduced by AAA protocols like TACACS+ must be carefully evaluated to avoid compromising system performance or response times, which are critical in real-time control applications. Lightweight and optimized implementations, along with thoughtful placement of TACACS+ servers closer to the industrial edge, can help mitigate these risks while preserving the advantages of centralized access control.

Another factor to consider is the cultural and organizational resistance often encountered when introducing IT security practices into operational technology (OT) environments. Operators and engineers accustomed to direct, unfettered access to ICS devices may view centralized authentication as an impediment to efficiency or as an unwelcome intrusion from the corporate IT domain. Successful TACACS+ deployments require strong collaboration between IT and OT teams, fostering a shared understanding of the necessity for enhanced security measures in the face of evolving cyber threats targeting critical infrastructure. Training programs, clear communication of security objectives, and tailored policy frameworks that respect operational workflows are essential in overcoming these human factors.

Compatibility with legacy systems and proprietary protocols also presents technical obstacles. Many ICS devices may not natively support TACACS+, necessitating the use of intermediary solutions such as jump servers, secure gateways, or protocol converters to bridge the gap. These components act as enforcement points for TACACS+ authentication and authorization, ensuring that even older devices benefit from modern access control mechanisms. However, the introduction of these intermediary systems must be carefully managed to prevent introducing new vulnerabilities or single points of failure within the ICS architecture.

Regulatory and industry standards increasingly emphasize the importance of implementing strong identity and access management (IAM) controls within ICS. Frameworks such as NIST SP 800-82, IEC 62443, and the NERC CIP standards all highlight the necessity of securing access to control systems to safeguard against cyber-attacks, insider threats, and accidental misuse. TACACS+ provides a practical and widely accepted method for meeting these requirements, aligning ICS environments with industry best practices while strengthening resilience against an increasingly complex threat landscape.

Ultimately, the successful implementation of TACACS+ within ICS environments hinges on a nuanced understanding of both the technical and operational dynamics at play. Security measures must be seamlessly integrated into the existing ecosystem without undermining the primary mission of ensuring safe, reliable, and continuous industrial operations. By balancing centralized control with operational flexibility, organizations can leverage TACACS+ to enhance security, meet regulatory demands, and protect the vital processes that underpin modern society.

Future of TACACS+ in Hybrid and Multi-Cloud Networks

The evolution of network architectures toward hybrid and multi-cloud environments has significantly altered the landscape of identity and access management, bringing new challenges and opportunities for protocols such as Terminal Access Controller Access-Control System Plus (TACACS+). Originally designed to secure and manage access to network devices within traditional, centralized infrastructures, TACACS+ now finds itself adapting to a world where resources and workloads are increasingly distributed across on-premises data centers, private clouds, and multiple public cloud platforms. As organizations embrace hybrid and multi-cloud strategies to achieve greater flexibility, scalability, and resilience, the role of TACACS+ is undergoing a transformation to remain relevant in securing these modern architectures.

The core functions of TACACS+, which include centralized authentication, authorization, and accounting, continue to hold significant value in hybrid and multi-cloud scenarios. However, the decentralized nature of these environments introduces a level of complexity that requires TACACS+ to evolve in its deployment models and interoperability. Enterprises are now faced with managing access control for users and administrators across a broad array of platforms, including traditional network appliances, virtualized network functions, containerized workloads, cloud-native services, and software-defined infrastructures. The ability to maintain a consistent and centralized policy enforcement point for these diverse assets is critical to reducing security risks and operational inefficiencies.

One of the emerging trends in the adoption of TACACS+ in hybrid and multi-cloud environments is its integration with cloud-native identity services and modern authentication frameworks. Cloud service providers (CSPs) such as AWS, Microsoft Azure, and Google Cloud Platform offer their own identity and access management (IAM) solutions, which are designed to secure access to cloud-based resources. To effectively manage access across both on-premises and cloud infrastructures, organizations are increasingly integrating TACACS+ servers with federated identity systems and Single Sign-On (SSO) solutions. By leveraging protocols such as SAML, OAuth, or OpenID Connect, enterprises can unify access control, enabling users to authenticate once and gain appropriate permissions across hybrid ecosystems, while still retaining the granular command authorization and detailed logging that TACACS+ provides.

Another critical area shaping the future of TACACS+ in multi-cloud networks is its alignment with zero trust security principles. As perimeter-based security models become obsolete in distributed and cloud-centric environments, organizations are shifting towards zero trust architectures, where every access request is continuously validated based on identity, device posture, and contextual information. In this context, TACACS+ serves as a valuable component in enforcing strict access controls at the network and device level. When combined with dynamic policies derived from zero trust frameworks, TACACS+ enhances the ability to limit administrative privileges, enforce least privilege principles, and ensure detailed accountability through its robust accounting functions.

Automation and orchestration are also driving forces behind the modernization of TACACS+ in hybrid environments. Infrastructure-as-Code (IaC) practices, container orchestration platforms like Kubernetes, and cloud automation tools are reshaping how network and security policies are deployed and maintained. TACACS+ servers can now be deployed as containerized services or virtual appliances within both private and public clouds, providing flexibility and scalability to match the dynamic nature of modern networks. Additionally, integration with automation frameworks enables the automatic provisioning and de-provisioning of user accounts, the synchronization of role-based access controls (RBAC), and the dynamic application of authorization policies in response to changing operational contexts.

The shift toward multi-cloud adoption also necessitates improvements in TACACS+ interoperability and standardization. Given the heterogeneity of cloud environments, TACACS+ must seamlessly integrate with a variety of platforms and network components, including virtual routers, firewalls, load balancers, and cloud-native network services. Open-source TACACS+ implementations and commercial solutions are increasingly supporting RESTful APIs, cloud-based logging services, and third-party integrations to facilitate this interoperability. This adaptability ensures that organizations can maintain consistent security postures across their hybrid estates, regardless of the specific technologies or vendors involved.

Security and compliance requirements remain a driving factor behind the ongoing relevance of TACACS+ in hybrid and multi-cloud architectures. Regulatory frameworks such as the General Data Protection Regulation (GDPR), Payment Card Industry Data Security Standard (PCI DSS), and the Health Insurance Portability and Accountability Act (HIPAA) mandate strict controls over access to sensitive data and critical infrastructure. TACACS+ continues to provide organizations with the ability to meet these obligations by enforcing granular access policies, maintaining immutable audit trails, and supporting secure encryption mechanisms during authentication and authorization processes.

However, TACACS+ is also facing new challenges in the multi-cloud era. One such challenge is the scalability of legacy TACACS+ architectures, which may not have been designed to handle the elastic and geographically distributed nature of cloud-native environments. Traditional TACACS+ deployments often relied on static, centralized server configurations, but the demands of global-scale hybrid networks require distributed and highly available TACACS+ instances capable of operating across multiple regions and cloud providers. Emerging solutions involve deploying TACACS+ as part of cloud-native microservices architectures, using containerized deployments and service mesh technologies to ensure resilient and scalable access control services.

Additionally, the increasing prevalence of ephemeral resources, such as short-lived containers and serverless functions, raises questions about how TACACS+ can continue to deliver granular control and auditing when assets may only exist for minutes or even seconds. To address this, forward-looking organizations are integrating TACACS+ with modern observability tools and cloud-native security platforms that can provide real-time insights into access events, automate policy enforcement, and dynamically adjust access controls based on continuously updated security telemetry.

As the complexity of hybrid and multi-cloud networks continues to grow, the role of TACACS+ will remain essential, provided that it evolves in tandem with the broader trends shaping enterprise IT. By embracing cloud-native principles, enhancing interoperability, and aligning with zero trust models, TACACS+ is positioned to offer a secure, reliable, and adaptable access control solution for the next generation of distributed infrastructures. Its ability to bridge the gap between traditional network security and modern, cloud-centric architectures ensures that organizations can maintain control over administrative access, protect critical assets, and foster operational agility as they navigate the challenges and opportunities of digital transformation.

Training and Awareness for TACACS+ Administrators

The role of TACACS+ administrators has become increasingly critical as organizations rely on centralized authentication, authorization, and accounting systems to secure their networks and infrastructure. TACACS+ administrators are tasked with implementing, managing, and maintaining access control policies that safeguard sensitive network devices and services. Given the evolving threat landscape, complex hybrid environments, and regulatory pressures, it is imperative that administrators possess not only technical proficiency but also a deep understanding of security principles and operational best practices. Developing effective training and awareness programs for TACACS+ administrators is essential to ensure the resilience and security of modern networks.

TACACS+ administrators must have a thorough grasp of the fundamental concepts behind authentication, authorization, and accounting. This includes an understanding of how TACACS+ communicates with network devices, how user credentials are verified, how access permissions are enforced, and how audit logs are generated and managed. Comprehensive training should begin by covering the technical specifications of the TACACS+ protocol itself, including its architecture, packet structure, encryption methods, and the differences between TACACS+, RADIUS, and other AAA protocols. Such foundational knowledge enables administrators to make informed decisions about configuring and tuning their TACACS+ deployments to meet specific organizational needs.

Beyond theoretical understanding, hands-on training plays a crucial role in preparing administrators for the practical challenges they will encounter in real-world environments. This includes configuring TACACS+ servers, setting up client devices such as routers, switches, firewalls, and network appliances, and integrating TACACS+ with directory services or identity providers like LDAP and Active Directory. Simulated lab environments, whether physical or virtual, provide invaluable opportunities for administrators to experiment with various configurations, troubleshoot common issues, and become familiar with command-line tools and graphical user interfaces used to manage TACACS+ servers and clients.

Security awareness is a key component of training programs for TACACS+ administrators. As custodians of a system that controls privileged access to critical network assets, these professionals must understand the potential security risks and threats that can arise from misconfigurations, weak policies, or operational negligence. Training should cover topics such as the principle of least privilege, secure password policies, multi-factor authentication (MFA) integration, and the importance of encrypting TACACS+ traffic to prevent interception and tampering. By internalizing these security concepts, administrators can better protect the integrity of their access control infrastructure and prevent unauthorized access to sensitive systems.

Incident response readiness is another essential skill for TACACS+ administrators. Training should prepare them to recognize indicators of compromise, interpret TACACS+ logs for signs of malicious or suspicious activity, and respond appropriately to security incidents. This involves understanding how to correlate log data with other security tools such as SIEM platforms, intrusion detection systems (IDS), and endpoint detection and response (EDR) solutions. Administrators should be well-versed in how to isolate affected devices, revoke compromised credentials, and restore secure access control mechanisms without causing unnecessary disruption to business operations.

Given the increasing adoption of hybrid and multi-cloud environments, TACACS+ administrators must also stay current with how TACACS+ integrates into modern IT ecosystems. Training should include modules on deploying TACACS+ in virtualized and cloud environments, integrating with SSO solutions, and automating access control workflows using APIs or infrastructure-as-code principles. Awareness of emerging trends such as zero trust security models, micro-segmentation, and cloud-native security services will enable administrators to position TACACS+ effectively within evolving enterprise architectures.

Communication and collaboration skills are equally important for TACACS+ administrators. They must frequently coordinate with network engineers, cybersecurity teams, compliance officers, and operational technology personnel to ensure that access control policies align with organizational objectives and regulatory requirements. Training programs should emphasize the importance of documenting configurations, maintaining clear and auditable change management records, and participating in security governance processes. By fostering strong communication channels and shared understanding across teams, administrators can help bridge the traditional gaps between IT, security, and operational units.

Regulatory awareness is another critical area for TACACS+ administrators. Many organizations must comply with industry-specific regulations, such as PCI DSS, HIPAA, NERC CIP, or GDPR, which mandate stringent access control, user accountability, and auditability standards. Training should ensure that administrators understand how TACACS+ can be leveraged to meet these requirements, such as by enforcing role-based access controls (RBAC), maintaining detailed accounting logs, and enabling secure remote access for administrators. An awareness of how regulatory changes or updates impact TACACS+ policies is essential to maintaining ongoing compliance and avoiding costly penalties or security breaches.

Continuous professional development is vital in this field, as the threat landscape and technology ecosystem are constantly evolving. Training should instill a mindset of lifelong learning, encouraging administrators to pursue advanced certifications, participate in industry conferences, and engage with professional communities focused on network security and access control. Certifications such as Cisco Certified Network Professional (CCNP) Security or Certified Information Systems Security Professional (CISSP) can provide TACACS+ administrators with additional frameworks and insights for effectively managing access control in complex environments.

Finally, cultivating a security-first culture within the administrative team is paramount. Awareness programs should go beyond technical content to address the human factors that influence security outcomes. Topics such as the dangers of complacency, the risks of insider threats, and the importance of ethical responsibility in managing privileged access should be emphasized. Administrators must appreciate the critical role they play in safeguarding their organization's most sensitive systems and data.

By investing in comprehensive training and awareness initiatives, organizations empower TACACS+ administrators to operate with confidence, precision, and vigilance. These programs equip them with the knowledge, skills, and mindset needed to secure modern network infrastructures effectively, respond to emerging threats, and contribute to the broader mission of protecting organizational assets in an increasingly connected and complex world.

Creating a TACACS+ Deployment Checklist

Establishing a comprehensive TACACS+ deployment checklist is essential for organizations seeking to secure administrative access to their network infrastructure. A carefully crafted checklist serves as a blueprint to guide network engineers and security teams through every phase of the deployment process, ensuring that critical steps are not overlooked and that the final implementation meets organizational security and operational requirements. The deployment of TACACS+ involves far more than simply installing a server and configuring devices; it requires a strategic approach that aligns with network architecture, business objectives, compliance mandates, and security best practices.

The starting point for any TACACS+ deployment checklist is a clear understanding of the organization's network environment and security needs. Administrators must first assess the current state of the network, including the inventory of devices that will integrate with TACACS+. These devices often include routers, switches, firewalls, wireless controllers, VPN appliances, and other critical infrastructure components. An accurate asset inventory ensures that the TACACS+ deployment will be comprehensive and will not leave gaps that could be exploited by unauthorized users. Furthermore, understanding the network topology, including segmentation and trust zones, helps determine where TACACS+ servers should be placed to optimize performance and minimize latency.

A crucial early task in the deployment checklist is selecting the appropriate TACACS+ server platform. Organizations must decide whether to implement an open-source TACACS+ server, a commercial solution, or an appliance-based offering depending on their needs, budget, and technical expertise. Factors such as vendor support, scalability, feature set, and ease of integration with existing identity management systems should influence this decision. Once selected, the server operating system must be hardened according to security best practices. This involves disabling unnecessary services, applying the latest security patches, configuring firewall rules, and securing management interfaces.

Integration with identity providers is another key consideration. Most modern TACACS+ implementations are integrated with centralized directories such as LDAP or Active Directory to streamline user management and enable Single Sign-On capabilities. Administrators must ensure that the integration process is thoroughly planned and tested to avoid introducing authentication delays or failures that could disrupt operations. Mapping user groups, roles, and permissions within TACACS+ to directory structures is an essential step in enforcing proper access control policies. The checklist should include verifying that role-based access controls are clearly defined and aligned with the principle of least privilege, ensuring users only have the necessary access to perform their duties.

Network device configuration is another fundamental component of a TACACS+ deployment checklist. Each network device must be configured to recognize the TACACS+ server as its AAA source. This typically includes specifying the TACACS+ server's IP address, shared secret, timeout settings, and fallback authentication methods. To prevent potential lockouts or service interruptions, local administrator accounts should be configured as a backup in case the TACACS+ server becomes unavailable. The checklist must ensure that every device is tested individually to confirm successful authentication and authorization against the TACACS+ server, and that accounting logs are being accurately generated.

Redundancy and high availability must also be addressed early in the deployment process. TACACS+ servers should be deployed in a manner that avoids single points of failure. This often means implementing at least two servers in geographically diverse locations with synchronized configurations and load-balancing mechanisms. The checklist should specify verification steps to test failover functionality and ensure that devices seamlessly switch to secondary servers when needed. High availability also includes monitoring the health of the TACACS+ infrastructure, which requires configuring network and security monitoring tools to alert administrators of any anomalies or outages related to the authentication service.

Encryption and secure communication protocols are paramount for protecting TACACS+ traffic as it traverses the network. TACACS+ encrypts the entire payload of authentication and authorization packets, but it is still essential to ensure that the underlying transport network is secure. The checklist should include validation that all management traffic, including TACACS+ communication, is routed through secure management VLANs or VPN tunnels. Any associated web interfaces or management consoles used to administer the TACACS+ server must also be secured with HTTPS and require strong authentication mechanisms such as multi-factor authentication.

Another important aspect of the deployment checklist is logging and audit trail management. The accounting feature of TACACS+ generates detailed logs of all administrative actions performed on network devices, which are crucial for detecting suspicious behavior, troubleshooting configuration changes, and meeting compliance requirements. The checklist must include steps for configuring log forwarding to a centralized log management or SIEM solution, setting log retention policies, and validating that logs capture relevant information such as usernames, device IPs, executed commands, and timestamps. The integrity and confidentiality of logs should be protected through encryption and secure storage mechanisms.

User training and access policy communication form another critical item on the checklist. Administrators and other authorized users must be informed of changes in the authentication and authorization process, including how their access will be managed through TACACS+ and what procedures to follow during outages or failures. The checklist should incorporate steps for delivering training sessions or documentation that outlines how to request new access, report incidents, and follow operational procedures aligned with the newly deployed TACACS+ system.

Testing and validation represent a significant phase of the deployment checklist. After configuring devices, policies, and server components, a series of tests should be conducted to ensure the system functions as intended. This includes validating that users are authenticated correctly, that authorization rules are enforced according to defined policies, and that accounting logs are generated consistently across all devices. Negative testing, such as attempting unauthorized commands or simulating TACACS+ server failures, helps confirm that security controls are effective and fallback mechanisms are operational.

Finally, change management and documentation are essential for ensuring the long-term success of the deployment. The checklist must include creating thorough documentation of the TACACS+ configuration, including server settings, device configurations, access policies, backup procedures, and disaster recovery plans. Change control processes should be enforced to ensure that any modifications to the TACACS+ system are carefully reviewed, tested, and recorded.

A well-structured TACACS+ deployment checklist acts as both a guide and a safeguard throughout the implementation process. By following a systematic approach that addresses technical, security, and operational considerations, organizations can ensure that their TACACS+ deployment strengthens the overall security posture, supports business continuity, and aligns with industry best practices.

Managing Legacy Systems with TACACS+

Managing legacy systems with TACACS+ is a task that requires both technical acumen and a nuanced understanding of the operational constraints present in many organizations. Legacy systems, which often include outdated routers, switches, industrial control devices, and other critical infrastructure components, typically lack native support for modern security protocols and best practices. Despite this, many enterprises continue to rely on these older technologies due to the high cost or risk associated with replacing them. This reliance creates significant challenges when attempting to enforce centralized authentication, authorization, and accounting through a protocol like TACACS+, which is designed with modern network environments in mind.

Legacy systems may present limitations in their ability to integrate directly with TACACS+ servers. Many older devices were built before centralized access control protocols became a common standard in network security architecture. As such, these devices might lack the necessary firmware support or configuration options to communicate with a TACACS+ server natively. In these cases, network administrators must explore creative solutions, such as using intermediary systems like jump servers, remote access gateways, or network access control appliances. These intermediaries can act as proxies between the legacy device and the TACACS+ infrastructure, effectively enforcing authentication and authorization policies on devices that would otherwise be incapable of supporting them.

Another common challenge when managing legacy systems with TACACS+ is balancing security improvements with the operational stability of the environment. Legacy devices often operate in mission-critical roles within industrial networks, financial systems, or utility infrastructures, where availability is prioritized above all else. Any modification to their authentication mechanism or network configuration must be approached cautiously to avoid disrupting essential services. Network administrators must conduct thorough testing in lab environments that replicate production conditions before applying TACACS+ integration to live systems. This ensures that the legacy devices continue to perform reliably while benefiting from the added security and auditability that TACACS+ provides.

When legacy devices cannot be upgraded or replaced and direct integration with TACACS+ is not feasible, administrators frequently implement compensating controls to secure administrative access. These controls may include isolating legacy systems within highly restricted network segments, implementing strict firewall policies to limit who can access these devices, and using multi-layered security mechanisms such as VPNs and bastion hosts. While TACACS+ might not be deployed directly on every legacy device, it can still serve as the gatekeeper to the systems that manage or provide access to them. By funneling all administrative actions through centralized TACACS+-controlled points, organizations can enforce access policies and maintain an audit trail, even when the endpoints themselves remain outdated.

In addition to network-level controls, securing legacy systems with TACACS+ often requires careful attention to user and privilege management. Many legacy devices rely on simple username and password combinations for administrative access, with limited support for granular access control. TACACS+, however, excels at defining fine-grained authorization policies that specify exactly which commands or functions a user is permitted to execute. By placing TACACS+ in the access path to legacy systems, administrators can enforce these granular permissions at the network level, even if the device itself lacks the internal capability to differentiate between user roles. This approach reduces the risk of unauthorized or accidental configuration changes that could jeopardize the stability of sensitive legacy environments.

A critical component of managing legacy systems with TACACS+ is the implementation of robust accounting and logging mechanisms. Legacy systems often have limited or no capability to generate comprehensive logs of administrative activity. TACACS+, on the other hand, produces detailed logs of every login attempt, command executed, and configuration change initiated via authenticated sessions. These logs provide vital visibility for network security teams, enabling them to detect suspicious behavior, respond to incidents, and demonstrate compliance with regulatory requirements. Integrating these logs with centralized log management solutions or SIEM platforms enhances the organization's ability to monitor and protect even its oldest and most vulnerable systems.

Interoperability is another factor that must be carefully considered. Legacy systems may use proprietary or obsolete communication protocols that are difficult to integrate into modern network architectures. When deploying TACACS+ to manage such environments, administrators may need to bridge gaps between old and new technologies through custom scripts, protocol converters, or network translation devices. This process demands a detailed understanding of both the legacy system's functionality and the capabilities of TACACS+. In some cases, this may also involve working closely with vendors or third-party consultants who have specialized knowledge of legacy technologies.

Another layer of complexity arises from the human factor associated with legacy system management. Personnel who originally configured and maintained these systems may have retired or moved on, leaving behind undocumented configurations or tribal knowledge that is difficult to recover. Therefore, as part of the process of integrating TACACS+ with legacy environments, it is essential to invest in thorough documentation and knowledge transfer. Administrators must take the time to reverse-engineer device configurations, understand operational dependencies, and capture lessons learned during the integration process. This knowledge is invaluable not only for the immediate deployment of TACACS+ but also for long-term system maintenance and incident response.

Security awareness and training play an important role in supporting TACACS+ implementation within legacy environments. Administrators and engineers who regularly interact with legacy systems need to be aware of the risks associated with outdated authentication methods, unencrypted communication, and insecure administrative practices. Training programs should emphasize the importance of adhering to modern access control policies, using secure management channels, and understanding how TACACS+ enhances the security posture of legacy assets. Awareness initiatives can help foster a security-first culture and reduce resistance to adopting centralized authentication solutions, even in environments where manual practices have historically been the norm.

Ultimately, managing legacy systems with TACACS+ is a delicate balancing act that requires harmonizing security improvements with operational realities. While the limitations of older devices may prevent seamless integration, TACACS+ still provides significant value by centralizing authentication, enforcing granular authorization policies, and generating detailed audit trails. By adopting a layered approach to security that combines TACACS+ with network segmentation, access control intermediaries, and robust monitoring, organizations can better protect their legacy systems from modern threats while ensuring continued operational effectiveness. The adaptability and flexibility of TACACS+ make it a powerful tool in extending strong security controls to even the most outdated components of an enterprise network.

Incident Forensics using TACACS+ Data

TACACS+ plays a pivotal role in incident forensics by providing granular visibility into the actions of users who access critical network devices and systems. As a centralized authentication, authorization, and accounting protocol, TACACS+ generates a wealth of data that is vital for investigating security incidents, identifying root causes, and understanding the full scope of potential breaches. In environments where privileged users interact with routers, switches, firewalls, and other infrastructure components, TACACS+ logs serve as a primary source of evidence that can help organizations reconstruct timelines and pinpoint unauthorized or suspicious activities.

The forensic value of TACACS+ data lies in its ability to capture every administrative interaction with networked devices. Each time a user logs in, executes a command, or attempts to modify configurations, TACACS+ records this activity with precision, including the user's identity, the timestamp of the action, the originating IP address, the device accessed, and the commands issued. These accounting logs are invaluable when responding to incidents such as insider threats, external breaches, or operational accidents. By analyzing TACACS+ data, investigators can differentiate between legitimate administrative tasks and potentially malicious or negligent actions.

One of the most critical aspects of TACACS+ data in forensic investigations is its capacity to provide a detailed timeline of events. When an incident occurs, investigators often begin by establishing a chronological sequence of user activities to understand how the event unfolded. TACACS+ logs can reveal who accessed the network infrastructure at specific times, which systems were targeted, and what commands were executed. This level of detail helps incident responders map out the attacker's or insider's movements within the network, identify compromised devices, and assess the extent of the damage.

TACACS+ data becomes even more powerful when correlated with information from other security tools and systems. Combining TACACS+ logs with firewall logs, intrusion detection system alerts, endpoint telemetry, and network traffic captures allows for a more complete picture of the incident. For example, if TACACS+ logs show that a user successfully authenticated to a core switch at an unusual hour and executed a series of commands to alter access control lists, firewall logs might reveal subsequent traffic flows that bypassed normal restrictions. This correlation enables forensic teams to identify both the method of attack and its impact on network operations and data security.

The forensic process also involves identifying anomalies in TACACS+ data that may indicate compromise. Analysts look for signs such as access outside of normal business hours, repeated failed authentication attempts, privilege escalations, or the use of rarely invoked or unauthorized commands. TACACS+ allows for the monitoring of specific command sets used by administrators, providing visibility into actions like the deletion of logs, disabling of interfaces, or changes to routing tables. Such behaviors can trigger alerts or serve as red flags during post-incident analysis.

Beyond identifying malicious actions, TACACS+ logs can also help in understanding the human element behind an incident. Attribution is a critical step in the forensic process, and TACACS+ facilitates this by linking each recorded action to an authenticated user account. Investigators can determine whether an account was used by its legitimate owner or if it was compromised through methods like phishing or credential theft. In cases of insider threats, TACACS+ logs provide direct evidence of the individual responsible for unauthorized changes or sabotage.

In environments with strict regulatory or compliance obligations, TACACS+ data supports the need for demonstrable accountability and auditability. Regulatory frameworks often require organizations to maintain detailed records of administrative access and changes to sensitive systems. TACACS+ logs satisfy these requirements by offering comprehensive records of who did what, when, and where within the network. This level of documentation is crucial not only for internal investigations but also for external audits and legal proceedings.

An important element of using TACACS+ data effectively in forensics is ensuring that the logs themselves are protected and reliable. Forensic integrity hinges on the assurance that TACACS+ logs are tamper-proof and complete. Organizations must implement controls to forward logs to secure, centralized logging systems or SIEM platforms, with mechanisms such as digital signing or write-once storage to prevent unauthorized modifications. Maintaining synchronized time across all network devices and TACACS+ servers is equally essential to ensure that timestamps are accurate and trustworthy during incident reconstruction.

TACACS+ data also supports proactive threat hunting efforts. Even outside of active incident response scenarios, security teams can analyze historical TACACS+ logs to uncover patterns indicative of reconnaissance or lateral movement. By regularly reviewing access and command execution data, organizations can identify emerging threats, detect dormant malicious activities, and strengthen their defenses before a security event escalates.

Incident response plans should incorporate the use of TACACS+ data from the outset. When a security event is detected, one of the immediate actions for the response team is to review TACACS+ logs to determine whether administrative accounts have been exploited or misused. This step helps define containment strategies, such as revoking specific user credentials, blocking IP addresses, or isolating compromised systems. During the recovery phase, TACACS+ data continues to be useful by verifying that no unauthorized changes remain in place and that systems have been restored to a secure state.

The post-incident review process also benefits from TACACS+ data. After containment and remediation, organizations conduct lessons-learned exercises to evaluate the effectiveness of their security controls and incident handling procedures. By analyzing TACACS+ logs, security teams can identify gaps in access control policies, uncover weaknesses in user behavior monitoring, and recommend improvements such as tightening authorization rules or implementing multi-factor authentication.

TACACS+ is a foundational tool in building an environment where forensic readiness is a core component of the security strategy. Its ability to document user activities in granular detail, its compatibility with a wide range of network devices, and its integration with broader security ecosystems make it an indispensable resource for investigators seeking to uncover the full narrative behind security incidents. Organizations that leverage TACACS+ data effectively not only improve their capacity to respond to incidents but also strengthen their overall resilience against future threats.

Developing Custom TACACS+ Extensions

Developing custom TACACS+ extensions has become a vital strategy for organizations that require specialized functionalities beyond the capabilities of standard TACACS+ implementations. While TACACS+ provides robust centralized authentication, authorization, and accounting services for network devices, modern IT environments often demand additional flexibility, integrations, and tailored workflows. Custom extensions allow organizations to adapt TACACS+

to their specific security policies, operational needs, and compliance mandates, providing a layer of customization that ensures seamless alignment with unique infrastructure requirements.

At its core, TACACS+ is designed to be extensible. While it follows a defined protocol specification, the open-source nature of many TACACS+ implementations enables administrators and developers to modify source code, add new modules, or integrate external services to enrich the standard functionalities. Developing these custom extensions often begins with a deep understanding of the TACACS+ architecture, which involves the client-side integration on network devices and the server-side logic responsible for processing authentication requests, issuing authorization decisions, and logging accounting data.

One of the most common use cases for custom TACACS+ extensions is enhancing authorization mechanisms to support more complex policies than what is available out of the box. While TACACS+ natively allows for basic command authorization based on user roles, custom extensions can provide highly dynamic authorization frameworks that take contextual factors into account. For example, a custom extension could enforce conditional access based on time-of-day restrictions, geographic location of the administrator, device criticality, or even real-time threat intelligence feeds. By injecting external decision logic into the TACACS+ server workflow, organizations gain the ability to craft nuanced policies that reduce risk without introducing operational bottlenecks.

Another area where custom TACACS+ extensions provide substantial value is in integrating the protocol with modern identity and access management ecosystems. Many organizations operate in hybrid IT environments where cloud-native identity providers and on-premises directory services coexist. Out-of-the-box TACACS+ servers may struggle to fully integrate with these diverse systems, especially when dealing with federated identities or SSO workflows. Custom extensions can bridge this gap by incorporating additional logic to interface with identity providers using protocols like SAML, OAuth2, or OpenID Connect. These integrations enable TACACS+ to act as part of a unified authentication flow, where users can seamlessly access both network devices and cloud services using a single identity.

Custom TACACS+ extensions are also valuable in environments where regulatory compliance imposes highly specific logging, auditing, or reporting requirements. While standard TACACS+ servers generate accounting logs for every administrative action, organizations might need logs to be enriched with additional metadata or formatted in particular ways to comply with frameworks such as PCI DSS, HIPAA, or GDPR. Developers can create extensions to customize log output formats, tag logs with specific regulatory identifiers, or forward enriched logs directly to compliance-oriented SIEM platforms, cloud storage, or immutable log repositories. This capability helps ensure that TACACS+ does not only serve as an access control solution but also as a key component in maintaining auditability and demonstrating compliance.

Custom extensions can further optimize operational workflows by automating repetitive tasks or integrating with orchestration tools. For example, developers might build a custom module that automatically assigns specific TACACS+ roles based on user attributes fetched from HR databases or IT service management platforms. Such automation reduces the administrative overhead of manually updating user roles within TACACS+ and ensures that access control policies stay aligned with organizational changes. Extensions could also be developed to trigger predefined workflows when certain conditions are met, such as locking out accounts after specific unauthorized command attempts or sending real-time alerts to security operations centers when risky behaviors are detected.

Performance optimization is another driver behind the development of custom TACACS+ extensions. In large-scale environments, the volume of authentication and accounting traffic can place significant load on TACACS+ servers. By building custom caching mechanisms, load distribution logic, or lightweight authorization workflows tailored to specific use cases, developers can improve the responsiveness and reliability of the TACACS+ infrastructure. This is especially critical in time-sensitive environments such as financial trading platforms, telecommunications networks, or industrial control systems, where any latency in authentication and authorization processes could disrupt mission-critical operations.

Developing these custom extensions requires a thorough understanding of programming languages commonly used in TACACS+ implementations, such as C, C++, or Python, depending on the specific TACACS+ server software. Developers also need to be familiar with the server's plugin architecture or modification points where custom code can be safely injected. In addition to coding, extensive testing in controlled environments is essential before deploying custom extensions to production networks. This ensures that any added functionality operates reliably and does not introduce vulnerabilities, performance issues, or unintended disruptions.

Security considerations must be central to any custom extension development. Introducing custom code into a security-critical system like TACACS+ carries inherent risks if not implemented carefully. Developers should follow secure coding practices, including input validation, proper error handling, and avoiding hardcoded credentials or insecure communication methods. Additionally, any external systems that custom extensions integrate with must also be assessed for security and availability, as these integrations could introduce new attack surfaces if not properly secured.

Documentation is another essential component of the custom development process. Detailed technical documentation describing the purpose, functionality, and configuration of each custom extension helps ensure maintainability and operational continuity. Future administrators and developers must be able to understand and, if necessary, troubleshoot or enhance custom modules without relying solely on institutional knowledge. Clear documentation also supports audit processes by providing transparency into how TACACS+ has been tailored to meet specific business or regulatory requirements.

Over time, organizations may choose to extend custom TACACS+ developments further by adopting a modular approach. By designing extensions as independent, reusable modules, enterprises can more easily adapt to changing operational or security needs. A modular architecture facilitates the rapid deployment of new features, simplifies maintenance, and allows teams to incrementally enhance the system as new requirements emerge.

Ultimately, developing custom TACACS+ extensions empowers organizations to align centralized access control mechanisms with highly specific operational, regulatory, and security demands. It allows them to extend the utility of TACACS+ far beyond its standard capabilities, ensuring that it remains a core component of their identity and access management strategy, even in the face of evolving technologies and increasingly complex network infrastructures. Through thoughtful customization, TACACS+ becomes not just a protocol, but a tailored solution designed to protect and optimize modern enterprise environments.

Preparing for TACACS+ Certification Exams

Preparing for TACACS+ certification exams requires a structured and disciplined approach, as these certifications are designed to validate an individual's knowledge and skills in deploying, managing, and troubleshooting TACACS+ implementations in real-world environments. Whether the exam is part of a broader network security certification or a specialized credential focused solely on TACACS+ and AAA (Authentication, Authorization, and Accounting) protocols, candidates must develop a deep understanding of both the theoretical concepts and practical applications of TACACS+ within modern networks.

The first step in preparing for TACACS+ certification is building a strong foundational knowledge of the TACACS+ protocol itself. This includes learning about the protocol's architecture, components, and key differences when compared to other AAA protocols such as RADIUS or Diameter. A successful candidate must clearly understand the role of TACACS+ servers and clients, how TACACS+ handles authentication and command-level authorization, and how it manages accounting logs. Mastery of these topics ensures that exam-takers can accurately answer questions about the core functionality and security features that make TACACS+ a preferred choice for many network environments requiring granular control over administrative access.

In addition to understanding protocol fundamentals, candidates must become proficient in the configuration and deployment of TACACS+

servers. This involves studying how to install TACACS+ software on various platforms, including Linux-based systems and commercial TACACS+ appliances. Familiarity with server-side configuration files, user privilege levels, policy definition, and integration with external identity providers such as LDAP or Active Directory is critical. Certification exams often test an individual's ability to design scalable TACACS+ infrastructures that align with enterprise security policies. Therefore, exam preparation should include practicing server configurations in a lab environment, which allows candidates to gain hands-on experience with real-world deployment scenarios.

Network device configuration is another critical area of focus. Candidates must understand how to configure TACACS+ client settings on a wide array of devices, including routers, switches, firewalls, and wireless controllers. This includes learning how to specify TACACS+ server IP addresses, shared secrets, fallback authentication mechanisms, timeout settings, and accounting options. Exams often present scenarios where candidates must troubleshoot common client-side misconfigurations or optimize device settings for high availability and security. Practicing these configurations on physical or virtual network equipment builds the confidence and familiarity necessary to excel in the practical components of the exam.

Security considerations are heavily emphasized in TACACS+ certification exams. Candidates are expected to understand how to implement TACACS+ within secure network architectures, applying best practices to protect the confidentiality, integrity, and availability of AAA services. This includes encrypting TACACS+ traffic, securing management interfaces, enforcing strong password policies, and integrating multi-factor authentication where applicable. Additionally, a well-prepared candidate must be able to identify potential vulnerabilities associated with poor TACACS+ implementations, such as using weak shared secrets or failing to implement backup authentication mechanisms.

To reinforce theoretical knowledge and practical skills, candidates should leverage a variety of study materials and resources. Official certification guides, vendor documentation, and reputable networking textbooks provide essential background information and best practices. Online courses, webinars, and video tutorials from trusted providers offer interactive learning experiences that help explain complex concepts in an accessible format. Study groups, forums, and community discussions can also be valuable, as they enable candidates to exchange insights, clarify doubts, and benefit from the experiences of others who have successfully passed the certification.

Practicing with sample exams and mock tests is one of the most effective ways to prepare. These practice exams help candidates become familiar with the format, question styles, and time constraints they will face during the actual test. By simulating exam conditions, candidates can assess their readiness, identify knowledge gaps, and adjust their study strategies accordingly. Mock tests also improve time management skills, which are crucial when answering technical questions under exam pressure.

Another key aspect of preparation is understanding how TACACS+ integrates with broader security and network management ecosystems. Certification exams frequently include questions that test knowledge of how TACACS+ interacts with security information and event management (SIEM) tools, network access control (NAC) solutions, and incident response workflows. Candidates should be prepared to explain how TACACS+ contributes to audit trails, supports regulatory compliance, and integrates with incident detection and investigation processes. This holistic understanding reflects real-world expectations of network security professionals and helps candidates approach the exam from a practical and solution-oriented perspective.

Familiarity with troubleshooting methodologies is equally important. Candidates should be able to analyze TACACS+ server logs, identify common errors, and recommend solutions to authentication and authorization issues. This may involve diagnosing problems with server availability, resolving shared secret mismatches, interpreting accounting log anomalies, or addressing network connectivity issues between TACACS+ clients and servers. Hands-on troubleshooting experience enhances analytical thinking skills and prepares candidates for both the exam and real-world problem-solving scenarios.

Finally, candidates should approach exam day with a confident mindset, grounded in thorough preparation and practice. Reviewing key concepts the day before the exam, ensuring familiarity with the exam format, and practicing stress-reduction techniques can all contribute to improved performance. It is important to remember that TACACS+ certifications are designed not just to assess technical knowledge, but also to validate the candidate's ability to apply that knowledge to secure critical network infrastructures.

Through diligent study, practical experience, and a comprehensive understanding of TACACS+ within modern network environments, candidates can position themselves to succeed in certification exams and gain a credential that validates their expertise in centralized access control and network security. This preparation process also equips them with valuable skills that are directly applicable to securing and managing enterprise networks in today's increasingly complex and dynamic threat landscape.

The Road Ahead: Next-Generation Access Management

The landscape of access management is undergoing a profound transformation as organizations grapple with increasingly complex and distributed IT environments. Traditional approaches to access control, while still foundational, are being redefined by emerging technologies and new paradigms driven by cloud computing, hybrid infrastructures, remote workforces, and evolving cyber threats. The road ahead for next-generation access management involves a shift from static and perimeter-based models to dynamic, context-aware systems that integrate identity, security, and automation in ways that were previously unachievable.

At the core of this transformation is the movement towards identity-centric security frameworks, where identity becomes the primary control point for granting or denying access to digital resources. Unlike traditional models that rely heavily on network segmentation and physical boundaries, next-generation access management focuses on authenticating and authorizing users, devices, applications, and services regardless of their location. This shift is necessary as organizations embrace hybrid cloud models, where workloads and resources reside across on-premises data centers and multiple cloud platforms. In these environments, the ability to enforce consistent access control policies across disparate infrastructures is a top priority.

A defining feature of next-generation access management is its integration with zero trust principles. The zero trust model assumes that no user, device, or service should be trusted by default, even if they operate inside the organization's traditional security perimeter. Instead, continuous verification and validation are required each time access is requested. In practice, this means that next-generation systems will incorporate risk-based authentication, contextual access policies, and real-time telemetry to make access decisions. Factors such as user behavior, device health, geolocation, and network anomalies will influence whether access is granted, restricted, or denied. This context-aware approach provides a much-needed layer of defense against sophisticated attacks that exploit compromised credentials or insider threats.

Another critical component of the next generation of access management is the widespread adoption of multi-factor authentication (MFA) and passwordless authentication mechanisms. As cybercriminals increasingly target password-based systems, organizations are transitioning towards more secure alternatives such as biometric authentication, hardware security keys, and cryptographic challenge-response protocols. These methods not only strengthen security but also improve user experience by reducing reliance on complex password management. The integration of adaptive MFA, where additional verification steps are triggered based on risk signals, further enhances the resilience of access control mechanisms.

Automation and orchestration are also shaping the evolution of access management. The scale and complexity of modern IT environments make manual access provisioning and de-provisioning unsustainable. Next-generation solutions leverage automation to streamline identity lifecycle management, ensuring that users receive appropriate permissions based on their role, responsibilities, and business needs. As employees join, move within, or leave an organization, automated workflows manage the provisioning, updating, and revoking of access rights across all connected systems. Integration with human resources platforms, IT service management tools, and directory services ensures that access policies remain accurate and up to date, minimizing the risk of orphaned accounts or privilege creep.

Artificial intelligence and machine learning are emerging as powerful enablers of intelligent access management. By analyzing vast datasets of user activity and network events, AI-powered systems can detect patterns, identify anomalies, and recommend or automatically enforce access decisions. Machine learning models can identify deviations from established baselines, such as a user accessing systems at odd hours or from unfamiliar locations, and trigger security actions in response. These AI-driven insights not only enhance the ability to prevent unauthorized access but also provide valuable data for security operations and incident response teams.

Next-generation access management is inherently tied to the broader concept of unified identity platforms, where organizations consolidate multiple identity sources and access policies into a centralized system. Rather than managing separate access control frameworks for on-premises applications, cloud services, and remote users, organizations are adopting federated identity models that provide a single pane of glass for identity and access management. This unified approach simplifies administration, enhances visibility, and ensures consistent enforcement of security policies across the entire digital ecosystem.

Another trend defining the future of access management is the incorporation of policy as code (PaC) methodologies. By expressing access control rules and security policies as machine-readable code, organizations can integrate access management into their DevOps and DevSecOps pipelines. This enables security teams to treat access policies as version-controlled artifacts, facilitating collaboration, testing, and automation. Policy as code helps bridge the gap between development and security, ensuring that access management is embedded early in the software delivery process and that policies can be consistently enforced across dynamic cloud-native environments.

The shift towards decentralized identity (DID) systems also represents a significant evolution in access management. DID frameworks empower users to manage and control their digital identities without relying solely on centralized identity providers. Utilizing technologies such as blockchain and verifiable credentials, decentralized identity models enhance privacy and reduce reliance on third-party intermediaries. In the future, DID could enable users to present trusted, cryptographically secured identity assertions directly to services and applications, paving the way for more user-centric and privacy-respecting access management paradigms.

Cloud-native architectures are influencing how access management solutions are designed and deployed. Modern access control platforms are increasingly offered as cloud-delivered services, enabling organizations to scale their identity infrastructure on demand. Cloud-native access management solutions integrate seamlessly with other security services, such as cloud access security brokers (CASBs), secure web gateways (SWGs), and identity-aware proxies. This facilitates the implementation of security controls in multi-cloud and hybrid environments while reducing operational complexity and improving agility.

The road ahead for access management also places a strong emphasis on compliance and governance. Regulatory frameworks continue to evolve, requiring organizations to demonstrate how they protect sensitive data and enforce access controls. Next-generation solutions embed compliance controls directly into their workflows, providing detailed audit logs, automated reporting, and policy enforcement mechanisms that align with standards such as GDPR, HIPAA, PCI DSS, and NIST frameworks. By integrating compliance as a continuous process, organizations can ensure that access management supports both security and regulatory obligations.

User experience is also becoming a key focus of next-generation access management. Security must no longer be a trade-off against productivity. Modern systems aim to deliver frictionless user experiences through intelligent session management, seamless SSO integrations, and risk-adaptive authentication processes. Access management solutions are evolving to meet the needs of diverse workforces, including remote employees, third-party contractors, and partners who require secure yet efficient access to corporate resources from anywhere in the world.

As cyber threats grow in sophistication and IT environments become more fragmented, the future of access management will be characterized by continuous innovation, integration, and intelligence. Organizations must adopt forward-looking strategies that leverage the full potential of emerging technologies while maintaining a focus on scalability, compliance, and user trust. The next generation of access management is not simply about securing systems but about enabling business agility, supporting digital transformation, and creating resilient infrastructures capable of withstanding the challenges of an increasingly interconnected world.